I NEVER MET
A RATTLESNAKE
I DIDN'T LIKE

I NEVER MET
A RATTLESNAKE
I DIDN'T LIKE

A Memoir

DAVID CARPENTER

Thistledown Press Ltd.
P.O. Box 30105 Westview
Saskatoon, SK S7L 7M6
www.thistledownpress.com

Library and Archives Canada Cataloguing in Publication

Title: I never met a rattlesnake I didn't like : a memoir / David Carpenter
Names: Carpenter, David, 1941- author
Identifiers: Canadiana 20220217203 | ISBN 9781771872270 (softcover)
Subjects: LCGFT: Essays
Classification: LCC PS8555.A76158 I5 2022 | DDC C814/.54—dc23

Cover design by David Drummond
Interior design by Marijke Friesen
Cover and interior images by Shutterstock
Printed and bound in Canada

Thistledown Press gratefully acknowledges the financial assistance of the
Canada Council for the Arts, SK Arts, and the Government of Canada for its
publishing program.

 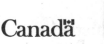

We are more powerful than ever before, but have little idea what to do with all this power. Worse still, humans seem to be more irresponsible than ever. Self-made gods with only the laws of physics to keep us company, we are accountable to no one. We are consequently wreaking havoc on our fellow animals and on the surrounding ecosystem, seeking little more than our own comfort and amusement, yet never finding satisfaction.
—YUVAL NOAH HARARI, *Sapiens*

What you call wildlife, we call relatives.
—OVIDE MERCREDI

This book is for Honor Kever,
my beloved partner at home and in the woods.

TABLE OF CONTENTS

INTRODUCTION

A Considertion of Creatures with Fangs, Claws, and Other Pointy Things

June 25, 2019

I am driving south on the Hanson Lake Road in our old vehicle. I go slowly, pulling a small wooden boat on a rickety trailer. My wife Kever is beside me, gazing to her left at the eskers that rise into a clear blue sky. Ahead and to my right, the ditch is green and grassy in the shade. A fallen tree in the ditch catches my attention. As we draw closer, the dead tree sprouts a sharp pair of ears. Feline ears. I am looking at the biggest lynx I have ever seen.

Closer still, the cat has expanded into yet another dimension, and I see the catface has shifted, displaying—*Kever!*—not the typical lynx markings (tufted ears, white beard at the throat), but symmetrical lines around the big cat's muzzle, descending on both sides of the nose like a misplaced handlebar—*Kever look!*—moustache, and a white furry mouth.

Kever says, *Where?* And we've already clattered past the cat.

In this old car with the rickety trailer, I don't like slamming on my brakes if I don't have to. I turn to Kever and I try not to stammer.

"It was a cougar."

Kever curses in wonderment and so do I, and I spot a place on the narrow highway where I can turn around.

"What are you doing?" says Kever.

I tell her I'm going back.

"Back there?" she says.

"At first I thought it was just a fallen tree," I say. "I memorized the spot."

"What are you doing?" she says again.

I gear down, turn partway onto a trail, check up and down the highway for traffic, Kever takes in a great breath, I ease the vehicle around, and I drive back up the highway. Not surprisingly, when I pass the spot, there is nothing left in the ditch, not even a fallen tree. A lynx might have held its ground because, most of the time, that's what they do. A cougar would have hauled ass.

One glimpse, no other witnesses. Visible for one glorious instant. Gone.

This book is about sightings of and adventures with predacious creatures (animals that prey on other animals) and all the excitement they engender in me, and, it turns out, a growing number of people. These encounters are hard to forget, and yet we do have lapses of memory, or we edit out details that might encumber a good story. In the telling and retelling of these adventures, we might go for the salient details, skip the boring descriptions, and heighten the dramatic moments; or, allowing our imagination to rearrange some of the facts, we come to believe that this is *exactly* how it happened. Our partners will frequently and publicly edit our stories. Well, maybe not *your* partner. Saddest of all, over the many years, some of our adventures might slowly detach themselves from our brain and sink like doomed ships beneath our consciousness. How many grizzlies, wolves, wild pigs, rattlers or cougars have I glimpsed and forgotten or misremembered? Who knows? I've kept field notes for fifty years, and they help to buttress my memory, but much has passed unrecorded.

Soon, in spite of the Covid-19 pandemic, I must don my mask, venture into an outdoor clothing shop, and buy a pair of hiking boots. I've worn out quite a few pairs of them hiking in the Rocky Mountains, trekking across England, tramping on the prairies and up through the boreal forest, lumbering over the Appalachians, and sloshing through the rainforests of British Columbia's West Coast. When I find the right boots, I will feel somehow renewed for more winter walks by the river and, with any luck, more hikes through the Cypress Hills and the northern forests of my own province. With these new boots on, I might even feel a tad younger. And when at last, collectively, we have set the coronavirus on the run or in some way contained it, and as travel restrictions ease, I will look forward to more road trips with Kever, or with Will (our son), and with our trail-loving friends. We travel to places near and far, mainly to walk. If this sounds obsessive, well, you might be right. In this volume, there are many obsessions to come.

The focus of the book is on animals, big and small, that prey on other animals, the predaceous ones I've encountered when I've travelled from my home to walk through theirs: weasels, spiders, grizzly and black bears, otters, mink, mosquitoes, snakes, big cats, and much more. These encounters, however brief, were likely more remarkable for me than for them. My brushes with some of these creatures retain something of the original thrill, and perhaps these thrills, vicarious though they have become with the passing years, are the driving force behind this book, the force that led me to the real subject: the animals, their precarious hold on their endangered habitats; the things I've come to respect them for; and the reasons why we need to love and protect them.

I don't aspire to become another Jane Goodall or a David Attenborough (or a David Suzuki, Suzanne Simard, Ian McAllister, Elizabeth Kolbert, Maurice Hornocker or Dian Fossey). There is a long list of brilliant and devoted luminaries with scientific credentials, luminary status, and film crews. I applaud their Thoreauvian reverence for wilderness and their vigilant stewardship of wild animals. Perhaps enough of their attitudes and commitments have rubbed off on me that I want to join their force—a buck private, if you will, in the army of wilderness advocates. I'm a storyteller on a steep learning curve.

What I have become already is a rabid conservationist. This discovery came slowly to me, but here it is at last in full bloom. If you are also this way inclined, I hope you will join me in arguing locally for the preservation of our magnificent and most endangered carnivores, and for the preservation of their habitats. If the prospect of saving the planet or any part of it makes you feel helpless and tired, or if advocacy seems a bit daunting for you, why not try to do some serious animal watching? Why not take your binoculars to Grasslands National Park in Southern Saskatchewan? Or camp somewhere in the Rockies and (safely and respectfully) check out the bears in mid-to-late spring? I'm speaking here more of pleasure than obligation. Do it while you can, because the time on earth for these breathtaking, mythmaking monsters may well be fleeting, and if we don't honour and protect their habitat, this century could be their last. When the great apex predators die off, something vital inside of us will surely die.

I've been thinking lately of our ongoing yearnings for dinosaurs. We'll never see their like again, but deep down among the network of neurons in our brains, there must be a tiny region from which a weird nostalgia for dinosaurs emanates. If I had to bet, I'd say it was somewhere in the hippocampus, a part labeled *This Way to Jurassic Park.* We reassemble the bones of dinosaurs, we make toys and confections of them, books and movies about them. But when the last of our own apex predators falls to the guns of poachers and jet-set nimrods, we may well fall into a similarly gormless state of nostalgia. I don't look forward to that time.

Some of these creatures in need of our protection can be scary, and this is part of their appeal; they excite fear in us. Their terrain is a theatre of flight and predation, a world that demands caution from those of us who enter.

Even mosquitoes can be scary, and not just in the tropics. If a female mosquito wants to survive long enough as a larva, or long enough as a flying, blood-sucking, plague-spreading, reproductive insect, it must learn to be wary of dragonfly nymphs and dragonfly adults. Or maybe the word is "fear." They must learn to fear dragonflies to avoid being caught in the jaws of these helicopter-shaped predators.

Dragonflies, in turn, must be wary of garden spiders and their ingenious webs if they want to live to mate with other dragonflies. But to the dragonflies and spiders, garter snakes are serious predators. And garter snakes are frequently swallowed up by much larger snakes, bull snakes and rattlers, who rank as the terrifying dragons in their world of dry bush and desert. Dragons, yes, to their victims, but most snakes need to be wary of various other carnivorous mammals, from weasels to coyotes, if they want to bring the next generation of snakes into the world. And although coyotes may develop a fondness for rattlesnake meat, they have to fear wolves and marauding cougars. Cougars need to fear wolf packs, and these wolves, if they hunt alone, must in turn cede territory to the grizzlies that move in on their kills to steal their food. Black bears have been treed and sometimes killed by wolf packs, and must have a well-earned fear of grizzlies. Grizzlies too have their challenges with wolf packs and perhaps even polar bears in the north. And polar bears wandering inland in summer, weakened from eating too little, need to fear some of the larger Kodiak bears. Above all, these mythmaking, nightmare-inspiring apex predators must acquire a necessary fear of homo sapiens, the most rapacious species on the globe.

What an anxious existence these monsters must lead. They have no daily cat kibble or cans of dog food, no doting humans to coddle them along. They have no police to protect them, no medical professionals to tend to them when they are injured, no hospitals or long-term care facilities in which they can grow old and sleepy at their leisure, and then die. Their deaths are painful but mercifully quick. They can only comport themselves as fearsome carnivores until a bigger carnivore or a pack of carnivores comes along. Or until we come along.

The essays to come not only follow the chain of predation from mosquitoes to polar bears in habitats where hunger and territory dictate the rules of the game, they also memorialize these predacious ones for their beauty and for the fascinating cycles of their lives. The more we impinge on their territory, the closer they come to our dwellings. And the closer they come, the greater is the danger that they will be shot, poisoned, trapped, or flattened by vehicles. Perhaps, in some sense, they simply want to come home, and that home is the place—with our many roads, mines, oil rigs, clear-cuts, acreages, ski lodges, golf courses, theme parks, industrial suburbs, ranches, and farms—that has been taken from them.

CHAPTER 1

The Bad Bug

*K*ever and I take many a walk up north in the boreal forest. These days, she is even more at home in the woods than I am. Our cabin on Little Bear Lake is so far north of Saskatoon that, upon arrival, the seasons have regressed. These walks take us uphill from the lake along some favourite paths that lead to a series of ponds set in a marsh surrounded by black spruce and birch. We walk these from May to October, but in the warmest months in between, I faithfully spray myself with bug repellent.

Enter the villain, droning: the murderous *Culicidae* family. They come in clouds with no silver linings. Mosquitoes don't bother much with my wife, but like a horde of micro-vampires, they seek my blood at every opportunity. It has something to do with body heat and sweat. I'm not sure if the scientists who work to keep us safe from all things vampirical have come to a consensus.

Mosquitoes are at their most vicious in the evenings. They will also bite at night. And in the morning. And throughout the day. In my neighbourhood, the worst of these draculating fiends are the species *Culex tarsalis*, the main carriers of the West Nile virus. Their largest swarms arise from early July to early September. In my many hikes on mountain trails, I have discovered that hiking enthusiasts in the Rockies, along the West Coast, or down in the Blue Ridge and Smoky Mountains, are far less likely to encounter swarms of these and other mosquitoes. I envy them.

The male mosquitoes are quite harmless but the females of the family *Culicidae* are about as welcome to the party as the flu. In the warmest months of the year, roughly every ten days or so, they will lay batches of eggs in as many ditches, swamps, water barrels, rusty pails, and fish ponds as they can find. But to do so prolifically, to create thousands of flying needles like themselves, they need to bloat their bellies with the blood of mammals, any mammals. In this regard, our bodies are nothing more than gas stations for hemoglobin. Slap a blood-engorged mosquito, and effectively you kill hundreds more.

In the summer of 2018, Kever and I had some friends visit us for a few days up north. One night, inside the cabin, the mosquitoes invaded, and their air raids were so relentless that we had to pull the sheets over our heads to get any sleep. On the following morning we tried to find their point of entry. The windows? The doors? A crack somewhere? That evening our cabin was again whining with them in uncountable numbers. It was scary, like a tribute night for Bela Lugosi.

I think it was Kever who finally spotted it: the grate on our wood stove. The weather had been warm, so we weren't using the stove. Some ingenious little bugger had discovered our chimney and summoned her buddies down the stack and through the openings in the grate to swarm into that sumptuous enclosure of human flesh. The swatters, they would call us. *Let's go get the swatters.*

I set a fire in the stove and stemmed the attack, and later I closed the grate. We swatted away at the remaining mosquitoes that sweaty night, reducing their numbers by dozens, but the other ten thousand or so enjoyed a merry time with us.

Significant fact: Around the year 1900, Nikolai Rimsky-Korsakov composed a classical piece "Hummelflug" that mimicked the sound of a bee. His "Flight of the Bumblebee" became so popular during the twentieth century that it entered into the pop music repertoire. There have been countless covers of this melody—and why not? It reminds us of bees, and bees are more than just stinging creatures. They are among nature's most beloved musicians, and they produce honey.

No one has yet composed a song to mimic the whine of the mosquito. You can look it up.

Mosquitoes are responsible for an appalling number of deaths throughout the planet—until recently, more than a million people annually. In 2018, the figure dropped to about eight hundred and thirty thousand deaths per year, many of them occurring, as usual, in tropical regions. The Zika virus, transmitted mostly by *Aedes* mosquitoes, seems to have hit Brazil the hardest. The mortality of those afflicted has been around one in twelve. Dengue has spread throughout some Asian and Latin American countries, where about half of the world's population is at risk. Between one hundred thousand to four hundred thousand people have fallen annually to what is referred to as *severe dengue.* This disease is spread primarily by the *Aedes aegypti* mosquitoes and to a lesser degree by the *Aedes albopictus.* Instances of dengue have grown dramatically in recent decades. Yellow fever averages about two hundred thousand cases annually, with thirty thousand deaths a year, mostly in Africa. In 2013, there were forty-five thousand deaths.

I should also mention that the *Aedes aegypti* mosquitoes, mentioned above, are such a scourge in the American South, especially in the Florida Keys, that an ambitious plan has been launched to wipe them out. A British biotech team is about to release some seven hundred and fifty million (harmless) male mosquitoes into the Keys. This hero squadron has been genetically altered with a protein that kills off female offspring before they become old enough to draw blood from their victims.

Further north on the continent, in 2018, twenty-nine Canadians died of West Nile virus. In 2019, eleven Americans died of eastern equine encephalitis. These and other diseases, such as the California serogroup viruses, are enhanced by climate change. The warmer our climate, the more extreme our weather events; the more extreme our weather events (for example, rainy seasons), the more welcoming our environments become to several dismaying species of mosquito.

The worst of all is the genus *Anopheles*, which is responsible for the organisms that cause malaria. The impact of the *Anopheles* has been so deadly for so many centuries that it has frequently changed the course of human history. As Timothy Winegard recounts in his recent book, *The Mosquito* (2019), malaria helped to repel the armies of Alexander the Great and to prevent his conquest of India.

Malaria was very likely one of the forces that discouraged Hannibal from invading the city of Rome. When the descendents of Genghis Khan were terrorizing Western Europe, they ran into a long stretch of rainy weather. Malaria-bearing mosquitoes may well have combined with an excess of sodden turf to force the Mongols to retreat. Malaria-bearing mosquitoes certainly delayed the destruction of the Amazon rainforests for many years. Hmm.

But don't let me catch myself going soft on mosquitoes.

In a world full of bad bugs, we bush-loving Canadians can be thankful there are forces aloft that are doing something about it. I don't mean pesticides. I don't even mean biologically-based pesticides. I know, I know—pesticide production is a multi-billion dollar industry. I am also aware that pesticides have saved countless human lives from mosquito-borne diseases all over the planet, and that they are widely used in support of better crops and healthier forests. But pesticide use has driven hundreds of weeds and hundreds of insects into evolving ever-stronger genetic resistances. Pesticides have managed to kill off an appalling range of wildlife, including helpful predators that would otherwise have helped to control invasive pests. And with the pests' growing immunity, you need to deploy more and more pesticides. Which means greater pesticide drift, more water pollution, more danger to the health of young children, and more environmental contamination.

During the early years of this millennium, the Bill and Melinda Gates Foundation endorsed and helped fund a safer solution: mosquito netting laced with an insecticide that kills mosquitoes. Since this discovery, about two billion such mosquito nets have been delivered all over the malaria-prone world. Reports from various outposts in Africa—where malaria accounts for about half a million deaths per year—tell us that this mosquito netting is being used for net fishing to stave off starvation. So the jury is out on how effectively these nets are performing, but the Gates' initiative sounds like a well-meaning step in the right direction.

In the ongoing battle against the baddest bug on the planet, I have a love–hate relationship with commercial pesticides and maintain a certain ambivalence for developed-country solutions to underdeveloped-country problems. But for the eternal superheroes of our troubled planet—bats, birds, spiders, and dragonflies, who eat mosquitoes—I have boundless admiration.

Bring 'em on.

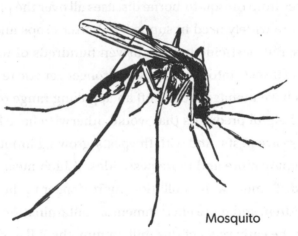

Mosquito

CHAPTER 2

The Good Bug

*I*t started with the usual routine. Chest waders, rubber flippers, Tilley hat, and life jacket. I call myself a fisherman, but on some days I look half frog, half man. I was trying for wily trout with little hand-tied flies and a rod that hasn't changed fundamentally in ten centuries. I'm an old-fashioned guy, so I don't care if I look like something out of a Monty Python sketch. The game is as follows: I will dress in silly clothes and try to catch a fish by stacking the odds against me as much as I can.

Once in a while, these trout lapse into blind, indiscriminate feeding, so once in a while, I catch a few.

On this day in late June, the weather was muggy and warm, the skies were turbulent, the wind capricious, and the clouds alternately fleeting or threatening.

The horseflies and mosquitoes, and their vicious squadrons, were everywhere, so as usual, I doused my exposed parts with the rankest of mosquito sprays, foolishly tossed the canister into the car, and churned my bellyboat towards the deep water.

The clouds returned and a prolonged roar of thunder exploded over my head—not a thunder clap but a thunder barrage, as though God were grumbling once more about the human race. Cautiously moving my fins, I kept within fifty metres from shore, just in case. The rain came slanting down, washing the mosquito spray from my face and hands. Because I'd left my mosquito spray container behind in the car, the mosquitoes went straight for me. Waving them off with little success, I cast my fly towards shore as far as I could and began to jerk my line in from shallow to deep. Up came the fly. I cast close to the weeds and cattails and then once more out into the depths. Nothing. An occasional rise out on the lake, well beyond where I was flogging the water. The fish were not biting but the mosquitoes were. The mosquitoes and the horseflies, two of God's great mistakes, were gunning for my hands and face. They seemed determined to bleed me dry.

I noticed a small commotion on the surface of the pond. I flapped my fins towards the spot and discovered a huge dragonfly floundering on the water. It had likely been caught in the downdraft from the perilous winds, and now it was drowning. I reached out and lowered my hand to scoop it up for closer examination. Before I could get my hand under the limp insect, it suddenly came to life, seized one of my fingers, and climbed onto my hand! A glistening dark alien, black and bronze with blue patches all the way up the fuselage—and I do mean fuselage. This dragonfly was almost eight centimeters long (three inches), a giant-winged raider in its own buggy habitat. Its wingspan was wider than my hand and its eyes were enormous. I tried to ease the dragonfly from me to the float tube, but it clung to my hand like a rescued cat for another minute or so. Then slowly it crawled onto the warm surface of my bellyboat. And there we were, two floaters on the pond of life.

The rain had stopped and the sun returned. In the presence of this wondrous great bug, I had forgotten all about fishing. I was caught in some kind of spell brought on by this biplane with enormous opalescent eyes. It was a lake darner, the biggest species of dragonfly in the entire boreal forest. And a small miracle immediately unfolded as the darner dried its wings in the sun: the mosquitoes had all disappeared. Even the horseflies had vanished.

Some of you readers will already know that no other creature in nature (with the possible exception of bats) has such an appetite for mosquitoes and flies. Black flies, deer flies, horseflies and hornets. If we just look at mosquito mortality, we discover that one hungry darner can consume hundreds of mosquitoes in one day. Up north in bog and fen country, you can walk around a mosquito-infested marsh, and if the dragonflies are out hawking, the enemy bugs will vanish. You don't even need fly spray.

Because of the charming monster riding along at my left hand, the enemy squadrons decided to retreat and torture other creatures, including my fellow anglers near shore. This analysis of mine is just guessing, of course, but it's an educated guess. I haven't yet, since then, tested my theory by leaving my bug spray behind. Perhaps my faith in dragonflies is not absolute. But that day on my float tube, the insects that sought my blood kept veering off into safer territory. The fishing was lousy but my new companion and I were enjoying the sun. Its wings were drying and its tail seemed to be twitching with pleasure.

Pleasure? How anthropomorphic of me. But something was happening here, something that I will never prove: I was apparently having some sort of relationship with this formidable bug. I had saved it from drowning; it had saved me from the dreaded mosquitoes and horseflies. We were travelling together, symbiotically, in quiet creaturehood. If at this moment the fish had begun to bite, I would probably have ascribed this good luck to the magical powers of my travelling companion. My albatross, my fierce angel. But on that day, the fish had something else on their minds.

Still, as I gazed ever so cautiously at the glistening tricoloured body next to my elbow, the compound eyes, the undulating blue-striped tail, the huge paired wings, the signs of its recovering strength, and the acquiescent attitude of its presence on my float tube, I was helpless not to ascribe something to it, something beyond mere bugness: my symbiotic traveling companion, my fellow voyageur, the comrade that I would try to describe to my wife when I got home.

I was resisting, of course, the fanciful temptation to call this mere insect, this thing with the face of an alien invader, my angel. Then I stopped resisting. This super-sized bug had become my official candidate for the angelic—and, just as the thought emerged, there was a whir of wings and the darner flew away. It didn't just fly; it rattled through the air like a marine helicopter.

❦

Let's say that you are me, with all my delusions intact. You are driving home to a cabin on a small two-lane highway. It's a long stretch, you're tired, and you're driving too fast. It's a warm evening and the little highway ahead is dotted with what look like broken twigs. But as you come closer, the twigs fly up at your approach. They fly up by the dozens, giant dragonflies basking in the late afternoon sun, taking in the warmth of the asphalt. Several of them crash into your windshield and, too late, you are reminded of your bug-eyed friend on the float tube of one hour ago.

What do you do? Keep on driving as fast as you can? Or do you slow down to allow the battalion of warriors to fly out of harm's way? The sun will soon be setting. In boreal forest country, you don't like driving in the dark and you don't want to get home late. Your partner is waiting. What do you do, oh ancient mariner, what do you do?

CHAPTER 3

Itsy-Bitsy Phobia

As with all observations of wildlife, you need to stand and stare. It is only when you stop to look that you will see what is around you. Quite often, it is when you stop for lunch and sit down that you will notice webs, a curled leaf, or wolf spiders sunning themselves.
—JOHN HANCOCK, *Spiders of Western Canada*

*W*hen I was about ten years old, my mother, my brother, and I were spending the last days of August at Lake Wabamun in a run-down rented cottage. My father was in the city working. One evening at the lake, my mother went off to a neighbour's cottage for a cup of tea. My older brother was somewhere up the beach or down the beach with his older friends. In spite of the growing dark, I grabbed a flashlight and headed down the communal path to find them. If memory serves me, I could hear their laughter and cavorting somewhere far off. As soon as I turned onto the path I came to an abrupt stop: there before me, as though hovering in mid-air, was a large spider. In alarm and fascination, I peered at the web that supported this creature, an orb-shaped net, woven like a bicycle wheel with the spokes meeting in the middle. The spider was parked at the hub of the wheel, and it was blocking my path. Legs included, it exceeded the circumference of a pop bottle cap, or even a Canadian half dollar. I could have run right into it.

I picked up a long stick. The spider was clinging to its web like an acrobat waiting for the fanfare to begin. I struck the web with my stick, tossed it away, and continued down the path.

It wasn't long before my flashlight picked out another big spider close to the path, and another. I found another stick and began lashing out at every web that blocked the path. Thus armed, I made my way towards the sounds of teenage revelry, but I never managed to find my older brother and his friends. My only big discovery that night was a fear inside of me that was vibrating out of control. I blamed the spiders because they looked malicious. Later I discovered that my fear had a name: arachnophobia.

Spider devotee Paul Hillyard (*The Private Life of Spiders*) claims that this chronic fear tops the list of animal phobias. A phobia, Hillyard explains, is "an anxiety or fear that is out of proportion to the danger of the situation." Its symptoms include "sudden apprehension, loss of control, shortness of breath, increased heart rate, faintness, sweaty palms and trembling." Fear of spiders is mostly irrational, because most spiders, even the huge ones, are harmless. Most arachnophobes know this already, but it doesn't prevent the loathing. It "awakes in them some primitive, probably innate, horror and repulsion that no argument can overcome." Hillyard goes on to discuss various explanations for arachnophobia, some arguing on the side of "innate instinct, genetically determined," and others favouring learned or acquired fear. These opposing schools of thought, and the research that supports them, have to some extent become gridlocked. Hillyard argues that the fear of spiders is not learned but innate: "Indeed, it is the state of *not being afraid of spiders* that is learned. An arachnophobic person is someone who has not yet learned to suppress, or overcome, the fear." The standard cure for arachnophobia is cognitive behavioural therapy, but, as I can affirm, the best kind of therapy is to read about spiders. Read about them, observe them. They are anything but boring creatures.

Spiders are everywhere. We know of more than forty thousand species, but many more have yet to be identified. They live in deserts, in houses, on mountains, in sewer systems, in the far North, and in other cold and barren rocky environments. They devour so many insects throughout the world that we could not do without them. But a few of them are scary for good reasons.

Australians have much to contend with in the venomous critters department, including *Atrax robustus*, the much-feared Sydney funnel-web spider. The females look like small tarantulas and have huge, downward-striking fangs. The smaller males are fast and aggressive against anything that disturbs their webs. The bite of these males is sometimes deadly because their venom (delta atracotoxin) is considerably more concentrated than that of the scarier-looking females. The venom of a male Sydney funnel-web spider interferes with the functions of the nerves, causing much pain, muscle cramping, shivering, and sometimes blindness. The toxin in this venom also brings about heart and respiratory paralysis, causing death—quickly for children and less quickly for adults.

However, these days in Australia, antivenom injections have become widely available, so the risk of death from a bite is much smaller.

South Americans frequently encounter two closely related versions of a venomous spider: in the north, the *Phoneutria fera*; further south, mostly in Brazil, the *Phoneutria nigriventer*. In some areas, they used to be called banana spiders because they were sometimes discovered in plantations, hiding in banana bunches. Now they are called wandering spiders. At their largest, these wandering spiders reach a leg span of twelve to thirteen centimetres (about five inches), roughly the size of a small tarantula. Unlike tarantulas, however, these wanderers are deadly, and they are even more to be feared than the Sydney funnel-webs. They frequently find their way into people's homes. They are fast, aggressive, and they don't back down from people who try to sweep them away. According to Hillyard, they will "leap onto, and climb rapidly up, the handle of a broom." Most of their bites are dry, but when they envenom their victims, their bite is extremely painful, causing tachycardia and arrhythmia.

In Canada, over the past five decades, no one has died of a spider bite. Near our southern border, across most of the country, we have black widow spiders.

Spider experts call these "northern widows," or *Latrodectus hesperus*. From my own observations, they appear to be the same size and bear the same patterns as black widows in the United States (*Latrodectus mactans*). Their legs and bodies are shiny black, like the sheen on patent leather shoes. On the bottom of their oversized abdomens is a bright orange hourglass design. Unlike those geometrically precise orb weavers of my youth, these big mamas spin large chaotic webs for their visitors. Although the widows seem to prefer dry rocky ledges in desert habitats, our largest widow colonies are found in the dewy mists of Vancouver Island. Sooke and Thetis Lake, both near Victoria, can boast (if that's the word) some of the biggest populations.

The female widow's bite is very painful and causes the muscles of the victim's abdomen to stiffen and cramp. The effects of the bite can last for several days unless the symptoms are treated. This near-galvanic pain should come as no surprise, as the widow's venom is considerably more toxic than that of a rattlesnake, One of their many favoured habitats is the outhouse, in which they may weave an enormous web spanning the hole. I mention this as a warning to all Vancouver Islanders—and men especially—who do their business in the good old house behind the house. Beware, men, of dangling in dark places.

Canadians might, very occasionally, run into violin spiders (*Loxosceles laeta*), also known as the Chilean recluse. This is a brown, relatively small, innocuous-looking spider with long thin legs. It has a violin-shaped pattern on the anterior part of its thorax. A few of them have been collected in British Columbia, and some spider experts claim they have been spotted in pockets across the prairies and farther east. Their venom has a toxic impact on our cells, and it leaves behind sores that endure for a long time. Like the widows, these spiders are most at home in desert and dry forest terrain. The above description also applies to a related venomous spider of the American Southwest and Midwest, *Loxosceles reclusa*, the brown recluse.

In an average year, six to seven Americans might die from a black widow or, less often, a brown recluse (violin spider) bite. This low figure prevails only because the antivenoms for black widows and brown recluse spiders are available all over the country. By comparison, in the United States between 1868 to 1968, there were seventy-two reported fatalities from *Loxosceles* bites. There were considerably more deaths from black widows during this time.

In Canada, arachnophobes have much less to worry about, except for black widows and a few large species whose hype is greater than their nip. The orb-weaving cat spiders (*Araneus gemmoides*), plying their trade from British Columbia to the three prairie provinces, are sometimes big and scary but harmless. The six-spotted fishing spiders in Ontario (*Dolomedes triton*) are big and sometimes aggressive, but also harmless. The hobo spiders in Alberta and British Columbia are aggressive, and their bite can cause headaches, nausea, and dizziness in a minority of cases. But their bite is not lethal.

Many a year has passed since my days at Lake Wabamun. I'm now a cabin owner up north in Saskatchewan's boreal forest, and there is an interesting array of spiders up there. We see ground spiders and runners in our woodpile, orb weavers in our woodshed and outside our cabin windows. I've found some large sheet webs in the workshop in August, which is mating season for many species of spider. In every mature tree on our property there are hundreds, perhaps thousands, of spiders. Each tree is a spider nursery and an insect graveyard for everything from mosquitoes to moths to horseflies, even the occasional dragonfly.

One of the things we love about our cabin is the chores: getting water from the lake, hauling, cutting, and stacking firewood, lighting fires, gutting fish, building or repairing things, getting the cabin ready in the spring and putting it to bed around the first snowfall. And we enjoy hosting our friends up at the cabin, the fishing trips and the communal meals. If you enjoy these things as much as I do, you have no time to indulge your fear of spiders.

I discovered this in my garage one day when a good-sized funnel-web spider of some kind was crouched on the cutting surface of my chop saw. I was so eager to begin my work that I simply reached over and brushed the spider away. Later, in the fall, I had to clean the leaves out of our eavestroughs, and several times I found myself staring at orb-weaving spiders—in my way, guarding their webs. Again, I brushed them aside with my hand—in this case, a gloved hand. But let me tell you, for a card-carrying arachnophobe ten feet up on a ladder, this is halfway to courageous. I had no time for my spider fear because I needed to concentrate on prying out the leaves. Around this time, I realized that somewhere over the years, I must have taken some kind of cure.

This cure must have started when I realized that I was truly interested in spiders. I took my own advice and began reading books about them. I learned that some tarantulas in South America, legs included, measured more than ten inches across, and that African baboon spiders could grow to eleven or twelve inches across. This reading was a delightful way of scaring myself, as children do, but my fascination with spiders gradually increased. I learned that spiders in their webs can send and receive sounds that are inaudible to the human ear, but they can be detected by artificial intelligence. These sound patterns, picked up on sensitive microphones, vary according to what the spider is doing—hunting, eating, or repairing its web, for example. I learned that the silk from some spiderwebs, measured by weight, can be five times stronger than steel.

Camping and hiking in Utah, my wife and I saw our first tarantulas up close. They were more fascinating than scary. By this time, I had stopped stepping on spiders in my home or in my way. They were doing good work by ridding our house of moths, houseflies, and other uninvited visitors.

That said, I don't think I'll ever handle someone's pet tarantula, or any other spider bigger than the width of a nickel. Like my mother, I like snakes and fear big spiders. My father was disdainful of my fear of spiders, but he had a snake phobia. My wife and I are somewhat similarly divided. We have a contract for camping in the desert: If a snake gets into our tent, I will handle it; if a big spider should enter, Kever will handle it. This contract has made for a beautiful relationship. And maybe, just maybe, the rattlers will leave us alone.

CHAPTER 4

Lo, the Serpent

Empathy is understandably a stretch when it comes to animals without fur or feathers, the more so when they lack limbs and moveable eyelids. Nevertheless, if people can begin to appreciate rattlesnakes, then turkey vultures and badgers should be easy.
—HARRY GREENE, in Richard Louv, *Our Wild Calling*

*O*ne cold morning in Saskatoon, Kever wandered up to my study. I could tell by the listless expression on her face that she was shack whacky. We had just endured five months of winter, and it was April. It was also snowing.

She said, "Let's go somewhere."

I looked down at my laptop as though it contained an answer to her plaintive suggestion. My laptop was stalled because my novel was stalled, because I was stalled. I asked Kever why we should go somewhere. After all, *I was writing a book*, for God's sake. Well, for my sake.

"Arizona," she said. "Let's go to Arizona."

She explained to me that when she had lived in Arizona, she never got to do any hiking. She fixed me in her gaze in order to drive home this point, and I broke out in a strategic yawn.

"There's wonderful trails all over Arizona," she said.

"Yep."

"There's rattlesnakes in Arizona," she said.

She brought this forth in a breezy, hopeful tone, and right then I stopped yawning. I glared up at her as she gazed out the window at the gentle, merciless flakes of April snow.

"You can see the rattlesnakes on the hiking trails," she said in a distant, meandering voice. "And in April, they're all over the place."

⁂

She had done this to me once before. This was a few years earlier. It was March and it was snowing. She'd been reading about the hiking trails in the Great Smoky Mountains. In Saskatoon, April would not be much better than March. The snow would gradually melt to reveal the cat piss and doggy doo and discarded drink containers and plastic.

"Let's drive down south."

"You mean all the way to . . . the *South*?"

Yes, that was the idea.

"What would it take to get you down there?" she said.

Did she not know that I was *writing a new novel*? That I was *fulfilling my destiny*? That maybe, just maybe, this one would *put me over the top*? An ingenious response to her came to mind. It had to do with Doc Watson, the blind and beloved musician from Deep Gap, North Carolina, who played old-time banjo and superb guitar. I had once idolized him, but Doc was born so long ago, he just had to be dead.

To Kever, I said, "If I thought that Doc Watson would be doing a concert down there, I would drive down south with you. Right now."

A while later, I was typing a long sentence which, I felt, managed to set the tone for a—Kever reappeared at my elbow, "April 26, Wilkesboro, North Carolina."

"Wha?"

"Sorry to interrupt you, but this is important."

I looked up at her warily. She was smiling and, oh crap, I knew what was coming. The guy had to be well into his eighties.

"Doc Watson is performing in a small music festival called *Merlefest*."

We dropped everything and to North Carolina we did go.

So this more recent time, the Arizona time, I was wise to her tactics. *But there were rattlesnakes all over the place.* Dammit, she had me once again.

Prairie Rattlesnake

I've always been crazy about snakes. My parents recognized this when I was seven or eight, so they gave me a snake book for Christmas. When I contracted scarlet fever and had to be quarantined in a hospital ward with a dozen or so other boys, I took my snake book with me. Every day for three weeks I read and reread it, and by the end of my quarantine, I had memorized the essential markers and habitats of about two hundred snakes from all over the world.

I didn't see a snake in the wild until I was ten. My father's company had granted him his first two-week holiday from work, and he drove the four of us from Edmonton to a friendly little resort in British Columbia known as Fairmont Hot Springs (now, alas, a mega tourist destination). My brother Peter and I learned from Mr. Bartman, the proprietor, that there were garter snakes living in the grass next to the swimming pool. My brother soon tired of this mad pursuit, which is what older brothers do, but I patrolled the wooden sidewalk beside this grass patch every morning until, finally, I spotted a small garter snake lying in the sun. This first sighting seemed to come with a bolt of lightning. I stooped to pick up the snake but it was too fast for me. It slid under the wooden sidewalk.

I was quick to learn a certain measure of stealth, and by the end of our first week in Fairmont, I had caught and released several garter snakes. One day I caught and released a rubber boa, the smallest and most northerly of the boa constrictor family. It is sometimes called the two-headed snake because its tail resembles its head. *What a find!* It was the peak experience of the summer, and a giant step for boykind.

I hated to part with the snakes I had caught, but I had nothing in which to keep them. After making some inquiries around the resort, I ran into one of Mr. Bartman's employees, who gave me a sturdy wooden box. It was a simple task to tack some screening over its open top, but a bigger task to convince my parents to allow me to bring some garter snakes home. Try as I would, I could not see their problem. I would give my snakes dirt and grass to crawl around in and leave a water dish for them to drink from. Handfuls of grasshoppers for them to eat.

"What if they got out?" my mother said.

"They can't get outa of this box."

She persisted. "But what if they get out of the box before we get to Edmonton? What if they find a crack or a hole or something?"

I was prepared for this question. My brother Peter and I had done some strategizing. In the last few days of our holiday, it was all I talked about.

"I could put the box in the back seat between me and Peter," I said. "We could check them every five minutes."

"I don't think your father would be terribly…pleased with that arrangement."

"You mean he's…"

My mother nodded. As a girl she had boldly chased her older sister around the house with garter snakes on more than one occasion.

"Painfully. Yes."

And there it was. My dad the athlete, the university football star, the fearless outdoorsman and surveyor, *who had camped in the woods in bear country and lived to tell the tale*, was afraid of snakes. I promised my mother that I would seal my snake box with tape and hammer more tacks to secure the screen. And so, bless them, they relented. Each night along the way, I opened the screen just enough to deliver the snakes various insect meals, and then I tacked the screen shut. We made the return trip to Edmonton without incident.

Back home I opened the cage almost every day and took my small friends out one at a time. I impressed my friends by letting the snakes crawl inside my shirt and out again. The neighbourhood girls were less impressed with this performance.

Coincidentally, when we arrived home in August, a circus was in town, and among the animals that travelled with the circus was a very long king cobra from India by the name of Claud. I pestered my parents to take me to the circus so that I could behold my very first venomous snake, but as things turned out, before our family could attend the circus, Claud the Cobra escaped, and for once in the city, everyone seemed to be talking about snakes. Search parties with dogs fanned out to find Claud, but for such a big snake, he turned out to be quite elusive.

One morning at feeding time, I opened the screen to find only three of my snakes in the cage. I think I assumed that the fourth was hiding under the grass and soil I had scattered on the floor of the box. But one day later, again at feeding time, I discovered that I had only two snakes. When my mother came to inspect the cage on the following day, there were none. With some alarm, she summoned me and showed me a small bulge on the screen between two tacks where the snakes had managed to squeeze out. My beloved garter snakes were out in the world once more.

On a Saturday morning in late August, I was lounging on the back lawn when I heard a terrible scream. It came from a yard three or four houses down from ours, a terrible scream followed by hushed and urgent conversation. That same morning, a van from the City Pound showed up on our street, and I put two and two together. If the city dogcatcher had stayed for any length of time, or had mysteriously disappeared, I would have assumed Claud the Cobra had crawled into our neighbourhood. But the fellow with the van had a brief conversation with Mrs. Crosby and drove away. I couldn't find the courage to ask permission to search Mrs. Crosby's yard for my escapees.

Several times, from late summer to early fall, I heard screams from various backyard gardens, and thus knew where my beloved pets were lying. By then, the story was out. David Carpenter had brought snakes home from British Columbia, and they had all escaped. Being just a kid, I didn't have much of a profile in the neighbourhood, but when my snakes crawled into the gardens of our neighbours, I became known as that boy who keeps snakes. Among the many victims of snake phobia in my neighbourhood, this was no compliment. But how could anyone lacking my obsession with snakes understand my love for them? Even boring old garter snakes were exotic to me. I would catch them, let them crawl through my hands and release them. But because I had spent most of my life well north of deserts and canyons, I had never seen a rattlesnake.

Much later, when I was a graduate student, I began to explore the Red Deer River country on summer weekends, and I came across my first bull snakes. These are much longer and thicker than garter snakes and more thrilling to catch. The ones I caught and released ranged from four to six feet. But what I really wanted to encounter, from a safe distance, were rattlesnakes. They were storied denizens of the American West and, unlike the garter snakes of my youth and the bullsnakes of my student days, they were *dangerous*. Kever, who had spent several years in Arizona, told me that she had a long history with rattlers. Had she invented this? Had I encouraged this invention? Why had I never cross-examined her on this herpetologist's haven?

The very day of her rattler revelation, I tucked my novel away, we packed the car, grabbed our passports, and off we drove to Arizona. Mile after mile, I could feel my resentment slipping away. Once we hit the lonely, snow-free highways in South Dakota, it was gone. I could finish the damn novel later.

In Tucson, we purchased some books on hiking trails and wildlife. When it was Kever's turn to drive, I read my way through Southeastern Arizona, bingeing on spiders and insects. Tarantulas were apparently harmless. In another book, *Venomous Animals of Arizona*, I discovered that the tiniest of scorpions were not harmless. In yet another book, I read that the emergency procedures for getting bitten by scorpions, Gila monsters, spiders, wasps, and coral snake bites always ended with the same advice: transport victim to medical facility. But what if you were camping away off in the mountains?

You may wonder why I wasn't reading up on rattlesnakes. Truth was, I felt I knew enough about them already. I just wanted to see one. And I realized by this time that spotting a rattler in the wilds might require a lot of luck. So, perhaps if I immersed myself in other species, I could broaden my expectations, thereby tempering my disappointment in case the rattlers failed to show.

For a change of pace I turned to roadrunners, scarlet tanagers and coppery-tailed trogans. We were not far from the Mexican border when I checked my insect guide for locusts. I remembered from something I had read as a boy that they could remain underground as nymphs for as long as seventeen years, and then suddenly emerge by the billions and destroy all the crops for hundreds of miles. My knowledge of locusts was perhaps more biblical than entomological. But our Arizona critters book revealed to me that there were such things as thirteen- and seventeen-year cicadas down here, so I hoped to see some. Apparently they emitted a high, whining sound, so we were likely to hear them, at the very least.

Armed with these factoids, ready for my first coral snake, my first Gila monster, my first tarantula—I set out with Kever on our first hike in Arizona. We were camped in the Chiricahua Mountains and had discovered a game trail that led uphill into a narrow, craggy gulch. We toiled up this rough trail for two or three kilometres, and the only wildlife we encountered were dozens of small lizards. Then we heard a sound: a high chirring call from the rocks along the trail ahead. A cicada was beckoning me! I got down on my knees, nose to the ground like a true bug sleuth, and peered around the rocks. Near a rounded rock, beside the trail, about twice the size of a stone hammer, I heard the cicada again, very close to where I was crouched. I peeked around the rock, and not far from my nose lay a rattlesnake, coiled to strike.

I don't remember standing up or jumping back. I simply found myself panting, and still crouching, a good six feet from the rattler. It was a very small snake, perhaps only thirty centimeters (one foot) long and light brown with a twin set of spots all down its back. Its rattle was a tiny affair that emitted a sound like that of an insect. The region in my brain where words issue had become wordless. All that remained was a giant neon sign saying *Wow.*

As we continued upward along the game trail, the brush and cactus had thinned out and the drop to our left became steep. What had been a hill to climb, with abundant flora, became a drier ecosystem, and everywhere in the crumbling wall to our right there were crevasses for the lizards to hide in. We were walking up through the beautiful remnant of what once was a mountain.

As the sun began to approach the horizon, we came upon another rattler, this one basking right out in the open over a precipitous drop to our left. It, too, was light brown and had the same pattern of twin spots down its back, but it was a much bigger snake, almost a metre in length. It was warming itself in the late afternoon sun, and it had what looked like a small swelling in the middle of its body, a recent meal, perhaps a lizard. Snakes like to lie in the sun after a meal, which is part of their digestion regimen.

To put it mildly, I was very excited. Two rattlesnakes, and I thought the thrill would never leave me.

The sun was setting when we started back to our campground. Darkness fell quickly. Knowing as I did that this was a typical hunting time for rattlers, this last half hour on the trail was a little nerve-wracking for us. I don't recommend nocturnal hiking in this terrain.

The following morning we had an enthusiastic conversation with a park biologist from Texas. When we described our two rattlers, the young woman's face brightened.

"You two are very lucky," she declared. "Those were twin-spotted rattlers, and they are very rare."

Her words gladdened me. At that moment, I realized we had arrived in a place far from home where, to some people, rattlesnakes were good news.

On another day during the same road trip, still in Arizona, we were heading towards some windblown mountains crowned with pine trees. Kever was driving along a small highway and decided to take a shortcut down a steep gravel road.

"Are you sure?" I said.

"Why not?" she said.

It was that kind of a holiday. Down we plunged over the white-hot gravel, clattering over axle-busting rocks. Towards the bottom of this incline, I finally exhaled.

"Well," said Kever, "that wasn't so bad."

I was about to disagree with her when I spied—could it be?—a big thick snake gliding slowly over the road, and owing to its great size, it was, unmistakably, the Tyson Fury of rattlesnakes: a western diamondback. It was so much bigger than our two twin-spotted rattlers that it made them seem like worms. I got out of the car and proceeded cautiously towards the snake.

More people have died from the bites inflicted by the western diamondback rattlesnake than any other snake in North America. The eastern diamondbacks are slightly larger and even more dangerous, but their numbers have declined to endangered levels in their traditional habitats in the American Southeast. The western diamondback, however, continues to prevail in small pockets throughout the Southwest and is still the most common rattler in the entire country. It has relatively long fangs for its size and a prodigious supply of venom in its glands. Occasionally they can be aggressive if threatened.

As I approached, the rattler continued to poke along. It crawled off the gravel road towards some clumps of sagebrush and cactus. It moved very slowly, as though to make a point. The toughest, surliest lout in the bar.

Speaking of excitement, I've been reading Austin Stevens' *Snakemaster: Wildlife Adventures with the World's Most Dangerous Reptiles*. According to one of the blurbs, Stevens is "known as an incredibly smart, yet incredibly insane animal lover." His stories, too, are "incredible." We are reminded of this twice in the same paragraph. "Sharing incredible stories of his love for animals and nature, this one-of-a-kind collection of stories will make you laugh, cry, and shiver with fear!"

I have to agree that his book has some thrilling moments, and it amounts to quite the spectacle. I will give you an example. Stevens agrees to help his friend Jack Seale, owner of the Hartebeespoort Dam Snake and Animal Park, to promote awareness and raise funds for the plight of African gorillas. To do this, Stevens agrees to spend one hundred days and nights inside a small glass and brick cage in the company of thirty-six "highly venomous African snakes." Stevens's roommates are six puff adders, six boomslangs, six black mambas and eighteen snouted cobras. The eighteen snouted cobras prove to be the least companionable of all the snakes. The first big problem comes with their discovery of Stevens's bed, which proves to be warm and comfortable at night. One by one, the cobras claim the bed and move in. Each night, Stevens has to remove all the cobras from his bed, then quickly jump in and settle himself. And each night, the cobras return to snuggle around his warm body. In order to prevent cobras from crawling up the legs of his trousers, he has to sleep with his pant legs tucked into his socks.

During Stevens's long vigil, a camera crew comes inside to film him and his friends. When the film lights are turned on, the snakes feel the warmth from the light bulbs and make for the lamps—and therefore the cameraman, who of course freaks out. One of the lamps collapses from the weight of too many snakes, and pandemonium breaks out. In Stevens's words, "the enraged serpents" begin whipping around the enclosure, "confused, frightened, and eager to kill anything that moved." The cameraman flees, leaving Stevens to fend for himself. He is now alone, "the only human resident in a cage filled with thirty-six highly venomous and extremely agitated serpents bent on revenge." One of the cobras joins Stevens on the bed and glares at him, with open hood, in strike position. Stevens wonders what "vindictive thoughts may be passing through its brain."

The reader will wonder where Stevens found the motivation—nay, the eagerness—to perform this "hare-brained publicity scheme." We hear very little of saving gorillas in this episode, indeed in this book, but we hear a great deal more about Stevens's nerves of steel and his desire to achieve the world record for days in a cage with venomous snakes. *Oh Lordy, why do I let these things happen to me?* He lasts for 107 days, gets bitten once by a cobra, and survives. In spectacular fashion, Stevens becomes the hero of his own story. He ends the action-filled chapter by reminding us, "To this day my record remains unbroken."

Gay Bradshaw has found a different approach to engage with and describe venomous snakes. In her book, *Carnivore Minds* (2017), Bradshaw reports that much recent research in reptile psychology has led to a new image of snakes. They display behaviour that reflects "higher-order faculties such as self-awareness and relational affinities." A male rattler will protect its mate by coiling on top of a female rattler so as to make her invisible to other males or other creatures. A pack rat and a rattler will sometimes hibernate through chilly weather by snuggling up together. Observations by rattlesnake specialists have led to the discovery of its "social sensibilities and ethical inclinations." Apparently, like bears and orcas, snakes adhere to rules of social protocol and manners that govern behaviour and relationships among the animals in their habitat. There is even evidence of what one might call an emotional life of rattlers, of which Bradshaw and other herpetologists find many examples. For instance, she cites a photograph of a male sidewinder rattlesnake embracing a dead female rattler that has been run over by a car. The original photographer is "hesitant to call it grief" and so is Bradshaw, but she doesn't rule it out. She tries not to ascribe a motivation to this scene. Like me, she seems in awe of the surviving male rattlesnake's posture of lying alongside and over the dead female. She sees this embrace as suggesting "sexual overtures" that might imply a desperate attempt to resuscitate the dead victim.

Bradshaw and some of her herpetologist colleagues regard rattlesnakes with what biopsychologist Gordon Burghardt calls "critical anthropomorphism" (Richard Louv, *Our Wild Calling*), a term that turns up more and more among naturalists and wildlife biologists. Much of Burghardt's work is on reptile behaviour. To understand the minds of serpents, he tells us that we "need to learn as much as possible about their abilities and sensory worlds; we need to know what brain structures underlie their emotions." If a snake is threatened, or scared, or hunting for prey—or simply hungry—something goes on in their brains and bodies that might be analogous to our own experiences when we are threatened, scared, hunting, or hungry. Burghardt would argue that they experience "similar—though not exactly the same—feelings that we have." This identification with their animal subjects contributes to our greater understanding of animals and "better scientific inquiry" (Louv, *Our Wild Calling*).

Rattlesnakes still flourish in remote regions of the United States, and, in an average year, five or six people will die from rattler bites. In

Canada, rattlesnakes are severely endangered. There are small populations of Massasauga rattlesnakes around Georgian Bay in Ontario, small pockets of prairie rattlers in Southwestern Saskatchewan and Southern Alberta, and equally limited populations of western rattlers (known also as Northern Pacific rattlers) in British Columbia, primarily in the Southern Okanagan. From my perusal of Canadian envenomation statistics over the past few decades, I could find no evidence of fatalities in either Saskatchewan or Alberta. In Ontario, there have been two fatalities, and in British Columbia, there has been only one. In my part of the world I've encountered much fear and loathing of rattlesnakes, especially in rural areas, but hardly any evidence of their having taken a human life.

There is one demographic on both sides of the Canada–US border, however, that seems susceptible to rattlesnake bites: young men. Most snakebite victims are males from their mid-teens to early thirties. Most of them are bitten on the hands or arms. I hope I'm not labouring the obvious if I deliver this warning: Don't try to be heroic in front of your friends by picking up a rattlesnake. Just leave them alone. For their sake as well as yours, leave them alone.

I am generally inclined to avoid torturing my readers, so I promised myself some time ago that there would be none of my poems in this book. Therefore, I apologize to my readers for the following momentary lapse. It's like bringing a banjo to a classical concert in hopes that the maestro might want me to pick a few tunes. The following is my tribute to the plains garter snake (*Thamnophis radix*). Like they say in the vaccination clinics, this will all be over in a few seconds.

Snake

Once   sewing a patch on the sleeve of an old shirt
I saw you curled at my feet

Later I found your hibernaculum
your family of gliding wonders

I learned to freeze and listen
every coil unwinding an elongated whisper in the fescue

you and your sisters wove
down the slope   around my sandals

black and yellow ribbons
flowing through parched grasses

Oh you are well worth my panegyric
Gaia's great glowworm fit for constellations

advancing your loops in a swift weave
to knit up the raveled sleeve of the world

CHAPTER 5
Chuga-rum, Chuga-rum

*S*o here we were once again, Kever and I in our little Corolla, this time driving south on the Natchez Trace, heading from Mississippi to Louisiana. I was wondering what a really big alligator would look like and how it might sound if disturbed. In our previous visits to the Deep South, we had come up with meagre results in our quest for finding big gators of the twelve-foot variety. I had read stories about them but I wanted to see the real thing.

I imagine that the paleontologists and taxonomists who have attempted to trace the evolution of the American alligator (*Alligator mississippiensis*) are sometimes perplexed by the many species of dinosaurs that resembled alligators and the true ancestors of alligators that looked more like dinosaurs. This quandary needed millions of years to get sorted out. Apparently, in the Jurassic period (two hundred million or so years ago), dinosaurs began to take their own dinosaurian path away from their alligator kin, and they went on to dominate their terrestrial habitats. In the same period, alligators began gradually to look like alligators: stubby limbs spread apart and flattened (as opposed to the locked-in legs of dinosaurs); long bodies and tails; flat and toothy snouts; and strong jaws good for snatching their victims from off the shore. Some of these alligator ancestors reached a length of forty feet and a weight of ten tons. Crocodiles and alligators, perhaps sensibly, retreated from the predations of the big dinosaurs to various marine habitats. When the great meteor struck at the beginning of the Cretaceous period (about sixty-five million years ago), the terrestrial dinosaurs disappeared while the crocs and gators survived. Only the super-sized members of their species were lost. Perhaps the most remarkable part of their story is that, from the late Cretaceous period onwards, the surviving crocodiles and alligators did very well and changed very little.

By the turn of our millennium, when Kever and I began our road trips to the Deep South, we had never seen an alligator in the wild. We had done some hiking in East Texas at the western edge of their habitat, and in North Carolina at the northern extreme of alligator habitat, and had never encountered one. But when we journeyed farther south, into the heart of alligator territory, we began to see them in impressive numbers. They thrived in the brackish waters of Southwestern Louisiana, in the estuaries of the Intracoastal Waterway, small ones up to three or four feet long.

But here we were, Kever and I, driving south on the Natchez Trace, about to leave Mississippi and revisit Louisiana. During a Faulkner pilgrimage to Oxford, Mississippi, and an Elvis pilgrimage to Tupelo, just an hour's drive from Oxford, we came upon the Natchez Trace, a gorgeous little highway for slow drivers and nature vultures like ourselves. We saw plenty of wild turkeys, lots of deer and squirrels, but still, at this point, nary a gator.

Another critter that I had somehow missed out on throughout my life was *Lithobates catesbeianus*, the legendary American bullfrog. I had read about them, heard stories about their voracious appetites, and even read recipes extolling their meaty thighs. I was told that, in Ontario, their mating calls could invade the sleep of cottage dwellers from blocks away. *Chuga-rum, chuga-rum and all that.*

Bullfrogs have probably commanded more attention from alligators than from paleontologists and taxonomists, but their evolution is just as interesting. Their presence on this planet appears to be much longer than that of the gators or crocs. The frogs' predecessors come from way back in the Devonian period, three hundred and seventy million years ago. The bullfrog is the largest frog on our continent, with a reputation throughout the planet for eating almost anything that moves, including scorpions, tarantulas, and venomous snakes—that is, snakes too small to make a meal of bullfrogs.

So here we were, in early April 2008, navigating the Natchez Trace, heading for Louisiana. We arrived late one day at St. Francisville, a lovely old town not far from the Mississippi River, and just a handful of miles into Louisiana from Mississippi. When we spotted the St. Francisville Inn on the main drag, we pulled over. The inn is an old mansion nicely shaded by big trees and crowned with tresses of Spanish moss. The Wolf-Schlesinger House, as local historians call it, had been a general store built between 1878 and 1881 by Morris Wolf, a Jewish merchant who had emigrated to Louisiana in the mid-nineteenth century.

During registration, we fell into a leisurely conversation with the proprietor, Patrick Walsh: where to eat in town, where to see the historic sights, and especially, where to go and gawk at bullfrogs and alligators.

Walsh smiled. "Well now, there's a question I don't get very often."

He told us about a pond just beyond the other side of town that harboured bullfrogs and a pair of alligators, among other critters.

"It's got a big old male that has a taste for chickens," he said.

"Chickens?"

"Yeah," Walsh said, shaking his head. "Teenagers like to drive by and throw frozen chickens into the pond."

He never explained to us how an alligator might nosh on a frozen chicken. Would the teenagers tear off the plastic wrappings first? Would the alligator wait until the chicken had thawed?

"You folks be careful now," he said. "Watch out for snakes. Don't go an' get yourselves bit."

We found the pond next to a dirt road just beyond the edge of town. We left the road and descended through trees along what looked like a game trail. We were scanning it for snakes when I heard a loud croaking sound. I wondered if I hadn't heard this sound before somewhere, when I wasn't looking for bullfrogs. Strange. That a bullfrog should greet us with his croak the very day, the very hour, we were looking for one. It croaked again, and true to its reputation, it was very loud. Probably not the fabled chuga-rum sound, but every bit as loud as reported. We descended, quiet and tremulous, listening for a big frog and looking out for an alligator. We saw neither, but again we heard that mighty croak.

They say if you stand still as a tree and just look, you'll see things. Kever and I waited, still as trees, for the big reveal. Along came an alligator, gliding slowly down the middle of the pond. It was about six feet long, probably the resident female gator we had been told about, which for us was pretty impressive. Perhaps she was looking for a nice bullfrog for lunch. Or at least a chicken.

While we were waiting to see if the alligator would find its dinner, I started to think how, in their own world, scorpions and tarantulas were scary-looking predators to be avoided. And the big bullfrogs in jungles all around the equator lapped them up like chicken wings. Eight-to-ten-inch bullfrogs are the *Tyrannosaurus rexes* of their neighbourhood. In Louisiana, an eastern diamondback rattlesnake or even a water moccasin might swallow a bullfrog whole. And a gator the size of the one swimming away from us might easily devour the snake. I wondered about the supergators of the Jurassic period, how poorly they might fare in a tussle with a tyrannosaurus. How strange, this ancient cafeteria called nature.

We moved on and I heard the croak again, but from much closer. It was not really a croak, much less a chuga-rum, but loud enough to send out vibrations in the air and tiny ripples on the water. It brought us both to attention. We crept forward near the edge of the pond, but not too close, knowing at last that this was no bullfrog. And there he was, lying in the shade across the pond, all twelve feet of him, dark green with ridges running like ancient mountain ranges down the full length of his hide, a survivor from a line that led back before all sapiens, all hominids, all mammals, to the steaming swamps of the Cretaceous period, an ancient brute lying in the shade and giving voice to his ancient appetite.

The alligator was going nowhere, but he seemed to know that we were the ones who had broken in on his slumber. Perhaps he was simply bellowing at us to back off. Somewhere between fear and reluctance, we backed away from the pond, and we lost sight of the great reptile.

Chickens? I wondered. A steady diet of frozen chickens? Probably anything of any size that strayed too near. A whitetail, a possum, a wild piglet, a bullfrog. Or a Canadian, simply looking for his first bullfrog.

CHAPTER 6

Popping Weasels

*L*ately I've been thinking about the ease with which people become associated with animals in casual conversation. *He's such a rat. She's a real fox. He may be gruff but he's really just a big old cuddly bear. Watch her when she goes for something she wants; she's such a tiger. He's a real snake in the grass.*

Many of these metaphors are gendered. If you're a man, and the people from your inner circle refer to you as a dog or a lion, you might feel flattered. But if the metaphor comes up *weasel*, you might not. A second definition of weasel is a deceitful, sneaky, or treacherous person (*Canadian Oxford Dictionary*). We weasel out of something by defaulting on an obligation. We weasel into something by cunning. Weasel words are deliberately deceitful.

Why should such a sleek, handsome, fur-bearing animal be treated this way by our language?

When we examine the predatory habits of the order *Mustela*, we encounter a rap sheet roughly equivalent to Mac the Knife. For example, in their pursuit of rabbits often larger than themselves, weasels leap, bite, feint and clutch with such frenetic energy they simply wear their prey down. The sudden appearance of a weasel can inspire such terror in a rabbit that it will freeze up and scream rather than flee or fight. One speculation is that some rabbits die of shock rather than injury (Elbroch and Rinehart, *Behavior of North American Mammals*). Like cougars, leopards, and lions, weasels often kill with a bite at the base of the skull. After severing the spinal cord, they feast on the brains of their victims. Mouse brains are their favourite snack. Could this be the reason that they are such villains in *The Wind in the Willows*? Poor rabbits, poor mousies. Poor gophers, rats, voles, and shrews.

But horror stories like these rarely take into consideration the body that impels such behaviour. Weasels are so long and lean, they are challenged mercilessly by winter. Their bodies are too long to allow them to curl up as do cats, dogs, and mice. Their bodies are also too long and lean to allow for any hibernation. To stay warm, weasels have to keep eating all winter long. Their metabolism is rapid, their heartbeat frantic. To stay fed, they have to adopt a mammal's version of the moveable feast: one to two meals per day, and for males, this means thirty per cent of their body weight every day throughout the winter. For the smallest of them, the least weasel, consumption amounts to about half of its body weight or more per day.

Weasels do most of their winter hunting at night beneath the snow crust. Their nocturnal eyeshine is an exquisite green. Their night vision is superb. Many years ago in the late fall, before I quit hunting forever, I was skinning out a deer carcass that my friend

Elsasser had helped me suspend from a tree. It was a warm afternoon in early November, and the deep snow had begun to melt. At one point, Elsasser was off tramping in a deep ravine nearby, and I thought I was alone. The work was going slowly but pleasantly.

I caught sight of a jerky movement about ten feet away, but the motion was too swift for me to make sense of it. These twitches at the edge of my vision continued until I halted my skinning activities. I waited a few minutes and at last I spied a tiny white head emerge from a hole in the snow, peering in my direction. It was a least weasel (*Mustela nivalis*). Although I had spotted a number of these tiny creatures rushing across prairie trails and roads, I had never until now locked eyes with one. With finger and thumb I flicked a tiny piece of deer meat in the direction of my onlooker. The little wad of meat seemed to frighten the weasel and its head disappeared back into the snow. But a few seconds later, the weasel popped up again, retrieved the slice of deer meat and hurried back into its hole.

Amazing. I had just been summoned to feed a wild weasel. I went back to skinning but stopped when I heard a faint trilling sound. Apparently my new buddy wanted another snack. I obliged with a tiny morsel. Then another. Five or six chunks later I realized that my weasel must be caching the food, not eating it. I continued to launch my little goodies. One of them flopped on my new friend's head, and it looked up and shrieked at me. Several times. Then it retrieved the offending bit and stowed it down in the hole.

Think about that. A seven-inch weasel had just hurled some weasel invective at me.

I had always thought of this weasel encounter as being meaningful: a hungry creature in need is helped along by another creature with plenty to give. Whenever I wondered about this unusual meeting, I assured myself that feeding a weasel out in the bush was nothing like tourists and their kids feeding junk food to bears along the highway. My feeding deer meat to a hungry weasel would not lead to the creation of habituated weasels. It was a one-off, a moment or two of recognition in which I fell into a nurturing role in service to a hungry animal.

These days I am less forgiving of myself, and I've become uncertain about the consequences of what I did back there in the Assiniboine River Valley. If all kinds of people, walking in the bush in winter, decided to feed every hungry weasel they ran into, would that not encourage habituation of weasels to humans? Would it not encourage weasels to lower their guard in the presence of any human being? Trappers, of course, might enjoy this newfound propensity among weasels to trust and seek food from humans. Therefore my good intention to help a hungry animal get through the winter could have resulted in doing it harm.

I still believe that there are ways of accommodating the wild animals that we have displaced without turning them into beggars and nuisances. I praise the heroic agencies that rescue whales, bear cubs, injured hawks, and abandoned fawns.

Many of the dedicated people who do this work try their best to reintroduce their recovered victims into wild habitats. They don't make the mistake of trying to *tame* them. That would be a sentimental lapse of judgment. Wild predators do not need us to try and become their friends. Forget all this self-gratifying stuff. If we really want to help these animals, what we need to do is move beyond our traditional role as habitual destroyers of wild animals and their habitats.

I left that encounter in the Assiniboine Valley unloved by the feisty little weasel, as it should be. Perhaps the best result of my encounter was that I managed, with the passage of time, to replace my stereotype of weasel-as-treacherous-brain-muncher with a creature worthy of my admiration.

CHAPTER 7

Saving the Cutthroat at McArthur Lake

*S*ometimes it's difficult for me to spot the difference between a pine marten (*Martes americana*) and a mink (*Neovison vison*). A large male marten can exceed a length of forty centimetres (sixteen inches) and tip the scales at two pounds (almost a kilogram). A large male mink can also exceed forty centimeters and weigh the same as a large marten. They are both brown. Owing to the luxuriant beauty of their fur, both species are trapped commercially. They are skillful predators and sometimes compete for the same small creatures to feed on. Neither one would hesitate to bring down a snowshoe hare. They are good swimmers and skillful at climbing trees, and both have a slight preference for hunting at night.

If I'm lucky enough to see these animals from fifteen metres or closer, I check out the ears and tails. The pine marten has big ears, shaped like those of a black bear, and a bushy tail. The mink has small ears and a slightly longer, less furry tail. The mink has a serpentine body and frequently arches its spine. Its pelt is the colour of dark chocolate. The pelt of the marten is lighter brown and its legs and tail are a much darker brown. The mink looks like the consummate, cold-blooded carnivore; the pine marten looks cute and cuddly.

Looks are deceiving. The pine marten is viciously territorial. When competing for mates, habitat, and food, pine martens frequently kill members of their own species. While the mink is also carnivorous, an adult is usually quite solitary and avoids excessive competition with other mink. The marten is semi-arboreal, and it even eats berries and nuts on occasion, whereas the mink is strictly carnivorous, and mink habitat is almost always close to marshes, lakes, streams, or the ocean.

The mink is much more at home in the water than the marten. In pursuit of fish and crustaceans, a mink can dive three fathoms and swim under water for a hundred feet or more. A mink lacks the speed of a diving otter but it does a pretty good imitation when fish are on the menu. I've seen mink many times hunting on lake shores for small mammals. Like otters, the mink seem to lack the shyness towards humans that other members of the family *Mustelidae* possess. I haven't often seen pine martens, perhaps half a dozen on the West Coast and only three so far in Saskatchewan's boreal forest. That's why I have no marten stories.

The domesticated version of the mink is readily associated with mink coats and, more recently, associated with the COVID-19 pandemic. It appears that domesticated mink living in close quarters with thousands of other mink in both North America and Northern Europe are susceptible to the same coronavirus that caused the COVID-19 pandemic. But my interest here is in the wild version.

෴

Here is a wild mink story that takes me back to the late summer of 1967, when I went camping with my friend Al Purkess. I had told him about the fishing, the hiking, and the alpine glories of Lake O'Hara, a small mountain resort west of Lake Louise, Alberta, where I had worked decades ago in the summers. This was in an era when lightweight tents and backpacks were not widely available. Had they been on the market, young guys like Al and me could not have afforded them. What we did have was a large canvas tent with iron frame supports and heavy poles, all of which we wrapped together and bound with a rope. We stuffed our packs with a few clothes, a case of beer (split equally), our food, and our fishing equipment, and we threw it all into Al's Studebaker. The plan was to drive to Yoho National Park and hike into Lake O'Hara, thus avoiding the bus that took tourists into the lodge. How hard could that be?

I must have failed to share this last bit of information with Al.

The road to the lodge and campground was six miles, much of it uphill, but what the heck, the first mile or so was the steepest. Among heavily burdened hikers, this early stretch was known as the Mile From Hell. I made a bargain with Al that if he would carry his pack *and* the tent with all its iron supports and half the beer up the Mile From Hell, I would trade him and carry the tent bundle the rest of the way. Al was bigger and stronger than me, so it sounded like a good trade.

We soon reached the beginning of the steepest grade, the storied Mile From Hell, a daunting sight when you're looking up at it. Al shouldered his pack and the big tent bundle, iron rods and all, and he lumbered up the steep road like the oldest nag ever to pull a milk wagon. I followed behind, lugging just my pack and a couple of fly rods, and as we tramped ever upward, I tried my best not to feel guilty over Al's burden. Was it wise to have brought twelve bottles of beer? At this stage of the journey, no, it was not wise. It was a dumb-ass decision. But if we were installed at the campground up above, each of us holding a stubby of Bohemian Maid, we would be applauding our wisdom.

An hour or more later, Al lumbered up to the point where the track leveled off. He released the tent bundle and it hit the road with an impressive *whump.* He sloughed off his pack full of beer and turned to me with a forlorn look. Sweat was flowing down his face like heavy rain. We extracted our canteens, sat by the side of the road, and drank.

Presently we heard the sound of a vehicle struggling up the hill. It was the Lake O'Hara Lodge bus, a multi-geared conveyance specially fitted for dragging tourists up mountain roads. The passengers gazed at us with what looked like bewilderment. For a moment, Al seemed puzzled.

"Carp," said Purkess, "that was a bus."

There was no way of arguing against this observation.

"Carp," he continued, "we could have been riding on that bus."

That was true enough. Tourists and hikers alike could buy bus tickets for the six-mile journey. But why *pay* to go up to Lake O'Hara? I was getting the feeling that Al did not share my frugality on this issue. Didn't *everyone* with outstanding student loans think this way?

I did concede, however, that Al might have a point.

I shouldered my pack and Al's dreaded bundle, and off we went. The road was still more up than down but the grade was considerably easier on us. We managed two more miles before we stopped again. I was determined to keep my side of the bargain, which meant three more miles of lugging the damn tent bundle.

We heard the approach of another vehicle, this time a gravel truck used for road repairs—an empty gravel truck. The driver stopped and gaped at us. About twenty minutes later, he dropped us off at the trail to the campground. Although we never parted with any of our beer, our thank-yous to the trucker were effusive.

The following morning a fellow camper, a former conservation officer, came up to us at the campground. He told us that the fly-fishing was good at McArthur Lake, and that in spite of the many boulders around the shoreline, one could cast from shore. McArthur, he told us, used to be a cutthroat trout lake, but during the early sixties, the fisheries crews had been stocking it with brook trout. These brookies had invaded the spawning stream and had begun to wipe out the native cutthroats by feasting on their eggs. He spoke *sotto voce*, out of the side of his mouth, as though imparting forbidden information.

"Take as many brook trout as you want. None of the conservation guys will ticket you."

He winked, one transgressor to another.

Al and I packed our lunches and our fishing equipment and began another vigorous hike. McArthur Lake lay up above the treeline. Without having to share the dreaded tent bundle, we managed the hike in less than an hour. The last bit of trail was downhill among big boulders and, in the bright sun, the lake was dark blue and clear, with many small inlets and coves, and a melting glacier at the far end. No one was around. A dozen or more brook trout were schooled up near shore, drifting into the shallows, and we watched them tail leisurely upwards, one at a time to the surface, to sip mayflies and caddisflies. We discovered there were also some larger schools favouring different inlets, so Al went his own way and I went mine. Al was still learning how to fly cast, and I offered to give him some pointers but he had probably had enough of my outdoor wisdom for a while.

The brook trout were obliging that morning. I could choose which ones to cast for, and if a small fish got there first, I would simply release it and try again. In one hour I had my limit of six plump fish, all around eleven to twelve inches. In the shadow of several boulders I found a darkened nook with a pile of crystallized snow. I gutted my trout, rinsed them in the lake and buried them in the snow. The next chore was to gather up the guts and bag them for the trek out, but when I returned to the darkened nook, I couldn't seem to find the guts.

Hmm.

Oh, well. I'd deal with them later.

I stowed my equipment next to the buried trout and went off to check on my buddy, who was two or three inlets down the lake. The first thing I noticed was that Al was casting like a pro. At last, Al had succeeded in casting a straight line without benefit of my instructions. He soon brought in a nice trout, and I couldn't help but notice that the ones he had kept were a bit larger than mine—which meant my supremacy as head fly fisher had fallen into doubt. But what an amazing morning we'd had! And we had also done our bit to save the McArthur Lake cutthroat. And in a few hours, we would be eating fresh brookies for supper by the campfire. Al followed me back to the inlet where I had caught my fish, and where my equipment lay next to the pile of snow. I was about to bag my six trout when I noticed that the pile of snow had been disturbed. There were faint traces of blood in the snow, but my fish were gone! After a bit of snooping around the rocks and boulders, Al discovered that my six trout had been moved to a recessed area beneath another boulder. I reached in and retrieved one of them, and handed it to Al. I reached for a second one, grabbed it by the tail, and encountered some resistance. A small furry animal snatched it out of my grasp. When I tried to grab for it, the animal arched its back and hissed at me.

Score one for the rodent.

Al and I sat on the rocks and had our lunch, gazing out at the occasional schools of brook trout as they rose for their own meals. We would return to our campsite and our bottles of chilled beer and feast on Al's trout for supper. I'm not sure we named our hissing adversary correctly at the time, but I now know that it was a hungry mink, who apparently had joined the campaign to save the cutthroat at McArthur Lake.

Mink

CHAPTER 8
Call Me Ahab

*S*ome years ago, I was paddling a canoe with two friends in a clear lake up north. They were trolling flies from opposite sides of the canoe and probably taking in the scenery when I spotted a beaver moving under water through a clutter of submerged trees. It moved labouriously, like an overweight scuba diver. Suddenly, it tailed to the surface, snapped up an insect, and glided back into the shallows. Okay, not a beaver. I dropped my paddle, grabbed the nearest fly rod and began to false cast over the heads of my two companions. I was spewing out cuss words in a manner that suggested a whole range of psychoses, and my two fishing companions reacted with some alarm. They needn't have. My demeanor was entirely understandable. The beaver in question was a brown trout about two feet long, and since that evening, it has grown considerably.

I was approaching my mid-fifties, and in spite of many attempts in the foothill streams of Alberta, I had never landed or even seen a porker brown as big as this one. My antics in the canoe spooked the trout (and my friends), and the fish took off in a burst of silt. From another canoe that same evening, my friend Cariou brought an eighteen-inch brown trout into the net. It weighed about four pounds. We all gazed at his fish as though beholding a particularly large emerald. I tried to pass off my extreme envy as admiration.

🐍

In their first year out of the egg, brown trout feed on larvae and insects: scuds, nymphs, mayflies, the usual trout fare. But the older they get, the bigger they get, and the bigger they get, the more predacious they become. Where I now fish, they grow larger than rainbows, which means that if you live in brown trout water and you happen to be a snail, small clam, small turtle, young mink, water vole, frog, duckling, crawdad, big leech, or small fish (including other trout), you had better watch out. After absorbing many tomes on the brown trout, written on both sides of the Atlantic—books that extolled the brown trout as the wisest, wariest piscine genius in the world—I knew I had to prepare myself for some serious predation. My own, I mean. Bringing in a brown trout of twenty inches or more on a fly rod, for me at least, would be the equivalent of climbing Annapurna in sandals.

The brown trout that fly fishers seek all over the country came to our continent around 1883, and to Western Canada from the United States in the mid-1920s. The breeding stock were frequently referred to as Loch Leven trout, and we associated them with

Scottish burns and clear English chalk streams. Crystalline waters like these may well have provided the habitat where brown trout learned their storied wariness. A trout in a clear stream running through a meadow is easily spotted by birds of prey and by human predators unless the trout learns to hide itself during the daylight hours—under a log, behind a boulder, or beneath an overhanging bank where they wait to ambush their prey.

There are still huge brown trout to be had in Scotland (Loch Awe, for example), but your chances of catching a big one on that side of the Atlantic are better in Norway, and better still in some remote rivers of Sweden. They grow bigger yet in the United States (Lake Michigan in the north, for example, or Arkansas's White River in the south). Your chances of catching big browns would be just as good in the rivers of the Russian tundra. But this would be a very expensive trip for non-Russians, involving helicopters and wilderness camping. So would a trip to New Zealand, where your chances of landing a whopper brown are even better. Wild brown trout grow bigger yet in the rivers of Patagonia, where you can still find the odd thirty pounder lurking around for something big to swallow. However, the prize for the biggest brown trout in the greatest numbers goes to some large lakes in Iceland, where anglers cast flies from shore for trout the size of salmon.

But what if your inclination is to fish locally? And what if you are more inclined to fish with wading boots or from a bellyboat than to use big fishing boats with big motors hauled by big trailers, which in turn are hauled by super-sized pickups? And what if you're not up for a lot of travel? You might be surprised to discover, from Newfoundland to British Columbia's west coast, the presence of brown trout lunkers near your home. Western Manitoba is probably the brown trout mecca for Canadians, but even in Saskatchewan there are half a dozen good brown trout lakes in the accessible mid-north and as many good creeks in the province's southwest. There are huge brown trout to be had in the South Saskatchewan River system, especially in Diefenbaker Lake. All of this testifies to the adaptability of brown trout. They occupy every continent on the globe except Antarctica. For centuries they have been the universal trout.

More than two decades ago, I was bellyboating with my friends Findlay and Calder in June. I was taking a break on shore when Calder hooked something. He seemed to be taking a long time with this one. From my vantage point, it looked as though Calder had hooked a sunken tree. But he persisted and finally netted a silvery brown trout hen about the size of one of his terriers. It was twenty-seven inches long.

Calder's catch was the culmination of many years of fishing for all of us, because until then, none of us had ever brought in a mega-brown. In nearly a quarter century of experimenting with various flies, various lines, exploring various trout lakes, trolling and casting flies in various depths, the best we could do was a couple of four pounders. On occasion we caught respectable brown trout, but we got skunked more often than not. Once Calder had opened the door with his huge trout, however, the whole gang of us was inspired to redouble our efforts to land epic brown trout. He had made Ahabs of us all.

❦

Animal welfare advocates, I imagine, are not easy on Ahabs. And
why should they be? We fly fishers are less culpable than hunters,
but only because hunters have not yet figured out a way to catch and
release the animals they shoot. Sometimes we use barbless hooks to
release our trout and thereby feel even better about ourselves. We
will also kill and eat some of our fish. Our moral dilemma goes like
this: we choose either to kill the fish that we claim to love or merely
torture it. Sounds like an old ballad, doesn't it? *Ah kilt the only one
ah loved / For she would not be ma bride.*

❦

A year after Calder's prize catch, we were back in our bellyboats. I
was casting a small fly that imitated a scud (freshwater shrimp), one
that I had used to bring in a six pounder. This fish had been stuffed
to the gills with scuds and a handful of two-inch minnows. On the
day in question, I had seen a rise about thirty feet from shore near
an abandoned beaver house. I had caught nothing that day, so my
casting arm was sagging with defeat. For solace, I was munching
on a chocolate bar. I stuck the bar into my mouth, cast the fly, let
out more line, and trolled the little scud into slightly deeper water.
Maybe I should change my fly for a bigger one? Munch munch. Maybe
I need a longer leader? Sigh. Maybe I should just turn around and
head for—

Something tightened my line and led it slowly away from the
shallow water. No jumping, no frantic runs to make the reel scream,

just a leisurely, prolonged bit of tugging, as though the thing on my line was as bored as I had been. Then, languidly, it descended to the bottom and remained there, immoveable, for some time. After about twenty minutes of log-like resistance, the fish came into view about fifteen feet from my bellyboat and an inch or two below the surface.

The George Foreman of all brown trout!

It was dark chestnut along the back, smoky yellow and spotted along the sides. Its fins were orange, and among all those spots were occasional blotches of red. This one was a male, and it had a formidable kype on the lower jaw, which in a month or so he'd be using to dig a trench for a female's eggs. His black eyes were ringed with gold. I realized he was looking at me, circling me, drawing me and my bellyboat around in orbit. He was too long and heavy for me to estimate his size.

Why was he not in a panic? Was he playing with me? Was he merely curious for a glimpse? Who was the top predator here?

We continued to give each other the eye as we went around and around. And then the fish stopped circling. As whales do when they roll from the surface to submerge, he parted from my fly, offered a departing wave of his tail, and faded into the depths.

Slow down, Carpenter, he might have been saying. *Chill.*

That's how big he was.

CHAPTER 9

Curiosity

*T*here is a string of clear trout ponds in the esker country south-west of our cabin in Northern Saskatchewan. Depending on such things as the lake's depth, the amount of flora, or which part of the spectrum shows when the sun strikes the water, the colour of the water differs from one pond to the next, from deep blue to pale green and much in between. These are the Gem Lakes. A hiking trail leads from the parking lot to Big Jade Lake, the first of the Gems, and it winds its way past the other five, including Little Jade Lake. Then the trail loops back. Anglers carry their equipment to the shores of Big Jade and either fish from shore or take a bellyboat or a canoe to go further into the system. Or hike in. The farther in you go, the more enticing are the scenery and the trout. But this is not a fishing story. No trout have been dispatched or otherwise abused in the making of this narrative.

Warren Cariou and I had been fishing the Gems since mid-afternoon. It was June, when the sun hovers late into the evening. We had lugged our bellyboats around the shores of Big Jade, flapped our flippers through Little Jade, hiked from the end of Little Jade to Diamond and Opal, and fished them both. I don't recall what the fishing was like; I only remember that when the sun went down and the twilight descended, we were both pretty tired. And so we began to bellyboat and portage our way back to where we had first entered the system. I think Warren was in front of me, but I don't remember.

What I do remember is a shape that appeared on the water, moving through the obscure light towards me. Not a waterfowl, but something larger. Bellyboats are inflated float tubes made of rubberized fabric, and therefore, I thought, fair game for sharp objects: the claws of a black bear, for example, or the incisors of a beaver.

Let's face it, all animals, including humans, are capable of territorial behaviour, especially at night. Even the herbivorous, industrious, boring beaver gets territorial when the sun goes down. But these were just night thoughts.

A mist had been rolling out over the surface of the pond, obscuring the outlines of the creature as it came nearer. Then, from a distance of about three metres, I heard a burst of nasal snuffling that made me churn my legs faster. The animal dove and then reappeared beside me, raising its head and sleek neck above the surface of the water, a mature river otter (*Lontra canadensis*), bent on escorting me away from its fishing grounds, or just checking me out. Perhaps both. I glimpsed its pale throat and its prominent whiskers, and God only knows what had drawn it to me. Maybe my super-sized flippers. I became aware that, for a long moment, the otter and I were caught up in our own curiosity. We were mutually engaged in watching each other. Nothing happened, but I'll never forget that moment.

A few years later, while Kever was paddling her kayak in the south end of Little Bear Lake, she spotted a romp of otters ahead of her. I'm speculating here, but it could have been a social group of bachelor male otters. More likely, it was a large family group of young otters with one or two adult females to watch over them. If the latter, it would have been quite a large gathering: four young ones, a mother, and a younger unmated female doing au-pair duties.

So here we have Kever in her yellow, banana-shaped kayak, peering at an otter family, who in turn are gawking at Kever. Then, all together, the otters approached her, six streamlined frolickers, their arched backs rising and falling wavelike through the water. They surrounded her and seemed to look up in wonder. In turn, Kever continued to gape back at them. I had felt lucky enough having a face-to-face encounter with one river otter, but I will likely never be as lucky as Kever was.

What continues to intrigue me is the otters' willingness to engage with Kever, until finally they swam away.

Whenever Kever and I rent our favourite cabin in the Gulf Islands in April, we spend many a watchful hour binoculating the cove from our front veranda. The eagles, kingfishers, and mergansers are fun to goggle at, and the seals put on quite a display, exploding out of the water to rid themselves of sea lice. But these creatures are no match for the otters, who swim (undulate, navigate, twist, swirl) rings around them. Over several years, I've watched individual otters mount the old wooden pier in front of our cabin and do their rolling and rubbing, a grooming ritual they perform to cleanse, dry, and renew their pelts. They do this with an abandon that approaches the erotic.

These west coast animals are also river otters. But I've also seen many sea otters (*Enhydra lutris*) out there. They are much bigger and fatter than river otters. A large male sea otter can reach forty-five kilograms. Together, floating on their backs like lounging tourists in lawn chairs, they socialize, feast, yammer, grunt, belch, and coo—all of this in flotillas of up to a hundred animals.

But river otters are my main interest in this chapter, partly because of the competitive terrain they inhabit and their conduct in this terrain. Competition can get vicious between rival carnivores vying for mates in season, or vying for prey. There are no absolutes of good and bad, only better and worse—by which I mean carnivorous animals that display more or less brutality in their competitive world. The weasel is a tiny terror, the pine marten is a regular Jack the Ripper, and the fisher is a gothic horror among the smaller members of the *Mustelidae* family. Badgers are big clawed and have a grumpy reputation. Wolverines can chase moose and caribou into the deep snow, where they wallow helplessly until the thirty-five- to forty-pound carnivore takes them down. Adult wolverines are also pretty hard on the kits of rival wolverines, and they routinely chase larger carnivores off their kills. In the hockey game of nature, these members of the *Mustelidae* family deserve a lot of time in the penalty box. On the other hand, the mink are skillful hunters but they are devoutly solitary and avoid territorial disputes whenever they can.

But among all the carnivores of the *Mustelidae* family, the river otter is the least competitive, the least inclined to violence, and the most companionable towards other mammals. These otters have even been observed sharing winter quarters with beavers in their lodges. But what I love most about the river otters is their curiosity and their willingness to engage with the most dangerous of creatures, by which of course I mean ourselves.

CHAPTER 10

Interrogating the Sphinx

*M*y wife is a great lover of trees. She lives by the mantra that trees are the lungs of the Earth. They are indeed the lungs of the Earth, but they are like reverse lungs: they absorb carbon dioxide and expel oxygen.

Back in 1998, we bought a shack on a long narrow lot up in the boreal forest (see Chapter 17, "The Cabin that Saskatchewan Built"). This shack, which we transformed into a cabin, was built on a disturbed piece of land with uprooted trees and a backyard that looked like a missile range. The destruction began with a leaky septic tank that had to be removed and replaced. Three times. The backhoes had scooped out the clay and deposited it on the top soil.

It lay in greasy, grey furrows where grass, bushes, and trees used to grow. For starters, Kever decided to plant the entire back lot.

A dubious enterprise as far as I was concerned, planting trees in such a dead space. These thoughts I muttered to myself, of course. Undeterred by this war zone, Kever went on a rewilding spree. At this time, she had become a Master Gardener, and she had already learned that once a patch of original prairie or wild forest had been ploughed or scraped, it could never be reproduced in its original form. But for Kever, this was not a deal breaker. A northern forest could at least be *approximated*. She began by digging in plant matter, fallen leaves, compost from our kitchen, and clods of uprooted grass and sedges. She also dug in ashes from our wood stove.

These additions, along with the few remaining weeds, would break up the clay and build up nutrients in the soil. In the same year, and in the following years, Kever bought some white spruce and aspens from tree farmers. She dug birch seedlings and willows out of ditches and rescued doomed wild berry bushes from wood lots. She planted them all over our destroyed backyard and beyond. From an earlier year, we had a large bag of peat moss that somehow captured a lot of seedlings blowing around in the spring. Carefully Kever lifted these trees-to-be from the peat moss bag and planted them with the other seedlings. I looked on in bewilderment as the luckless little plants were tucked into their new homes—and in greater bewilderment as many of them began to grow. In spite of the rabbits, the poverty of the soil, and many other things that might be daunting for skeptics like myself, our back lot, and patches of soil in the front and sides of our land, began to come alive. Things grow slowly up north, but at the time of this writing, some of Kever's trees have climbed to ten metres. Her raspberry bushes, saskatoons, bog cranberries, and blueberries have also grown to adult size, and their fruit has made our meals more tangy. The rabbits are still a challenge to some of her trees and bushes, but every few years, a lynx or two will move in and cull the rabbits. We've seen them on our land and caught them on our trail camera.

The good old predators, the fierce and vigilant predators, they are so obliging. They keep nature from running amok by culling animals that threaten to overgraze or overcrowd an ecosystem: mice, voles, squirrels, and rabbits, for example. Kever's rewilded lot attracted all these herbivores within the first five years of her planting, and just when the rabbit population began to soar, Kever's new forest attracted its first lynx.

🐾

I have a long, if somewhat remote, relationship with *Lynx canadensis*. It started in 1964 when I was back in Jasper, AB, living in a tent cabin on Lake Edith. Two friends and I had hiked upstream along the upper Athabasca River and camped near a warden's cabin across the river from Dragon Lake. When it was time to return, we hiked north along the same trail, heading downstream for Sunwapta Falls where we had left our car. About halfway along the trail, we came upon a lynx crouched in the middle of the path, effectively blocking our way.

We approached the cat and it didn't budge, so I was granted a good long look at my first lynx. It was not particularly large, maybe fifteen pounds, a drab yellowish brown, and it seemed almost excessively furry. Its forelegs and paws were very broad in relation to the rest of its body. The ears, of course, really stood out, with their foppish black tufts.

The cat continued to hold its ground, and I wondered if it had acquired some affliction, rabies perhaps. It didn't hiss or show its teeth; it seemed almost to be in a trance. If not rabid, was the animal defying us to take it on? Did it fear fleeing us? If it betrayed this fear by running off, perhaps it would embolden us to chase it? Was that why it held its ground, or was our lynx simply without fear, and therefore without any reason to give ground?

Another possibility was that the lynx had a litter of kits hidden nearby. Or maybe the lynx was guarding its latest kill, cached under a pile of leaves and branches. Or, was this animal too clueless to realize that the enemy was drawing near?

I may just as well have been wondering about a sphinx. We headed into the bush to give the inscrutable cat a wide berth, then returned to our trail.

Many years later in Northern Saskatchewan, I spotted a lynx hunkered down in a ditch on the Hanson Lake Road. I parked on the side of the road and approached it. Nothing. The lynx greeted me with the same indifferent attitude as the first lynx had, as though I were the biggest non-event of its day. Not long after that encounter I saw another lynx just off the Gem Lakes trail, and this one also held its ground, and it blinked its eyes as though contemplating a nap. As the years went on, I also witnessed a few lynxes that did move off at my approach, including a big one a few kilometres from our cabin. I have to wonder if this more prudent behaviour from the cats that gave ground was something they had *learned* from early bad encounters with humans. But really, I have no idea.

One warm evening in the early fall, Kever and I took a walk just as twilight was coming on. We chose a trail through the trees that we had often taken, one that led uphill to a view of the southwest end of Little Bear Lake. In the fading light we spotted a large cat coming our way, and at first I thought it might have been a young cougar. We stared at the animal until it was close enough that we could make out its stubby, black-tipped tail. Not a cougar, but a mature lynx on the prowl. It spotted us and stopped to wait on the path, staring at us, big for a lynx, perhaps twenty-five or more pounds. Then, placidly, the cat sat on its haunches.

What I remember most about this moment was the relaxed demeanor of the cat. It seemed curious about our presence on the path, but supremely unwary. And there we were, blocking each other's way. Kever and I decided to approach the lynx as though it were just a domestic tabby in our city neighbourhood. As we neared it, the cat drifted off the path and disappeared. At the place on the path from which the cat had exited, we peered into the bush. The lynx was right there, less than three feet from Kever's knee. I could sense Kever's fascination as we stood so close to the animal. My memory tells me that its eyes were greenish brown, but how could I have discerned that colour in the fading light? Worried that we had already violated the cat's boundaries, I put my hand on Kever's back and eased her forward, away from the crouching animal. We continued up the trail.

Sometimes in the fall, before the darkness has descended, I drive to Sealy Lake, not far from our cabin, to look for otters or to watch trout rise. One evening, Kever and I were on the pier gazing at the water. One of us turned around and there, perhaps fifty feet away, was a lynx sitting on its haunches checking us out. It had approached us out of nowhere. We returned its gaze and it looked away. At the bush, at the water, at us again. It remained there in that serene attitude for ten or fifteen minutes. Something caught our attention, perhaps the blurp of a rising trout. When we turned back, the lynx was gone.

It's a challenge to write about a non-event, even a wondrous non-event, when a sphinx-like creature appears and floats its riddles our way. What brought that lynx so close? What impulse led it to hold its ground? Why did it seem not to fear us? Did it sense that Kever and I were non-threatening? Was it simply waiting for us to get out of the way?

On this fall evening, what struck me was the confidence of the animal. After all, on occasion, lynxes do bring down and devour young ungulates such as deer fawns, elk calves, and mountain sheep. So there were reasons for the cat to feel confidence in proximity to big creatures like ourselves. But of course I can't be sure it was the creature's confidence that was on display. I can only speculate and hope for another chance to test my theory. Kever sets up our trail camera every spring in the North. Mostly we get images of snowshoe hares, but once in a while, another unknowable lynx will have prowled through our yard at night. Each time we see one on the viewer, we feel blessed.

Lynx

CHAPTER 11

Nocturnal Chorales

*The oldest language—all those patterns and signals we share
with other animals—continues. When we answer the call of
a coyote or owl with our own, we sing the oldest song.*
—RICHARD LOUV, *Our Wild Calling*

*I*n researching some of my previous essays on members of the
Mustelidae family, anything from weasels to wolverines, I was
surprised to learn how (excuse the adjective) licentious is their
copulating. Among the weasel family, during their brief seasons of
mating, it's rumpy-bumpy, jig-a-jig in all directions. By comparison,
coyotes are the supreme faithful lovers of the mammal kingdom.
They mate for life. This fidelity serves them well in their communal existence, where coyotes of both sexes tend to the litters. The
coyotes are great survivors.

By contrast, North American cougars have been extirpated from roughly two thirds of their historic ranges. There is reason to worry about their survival. I have no such fears for the survival of coyotes (*Canis latrans*), the ones in my province or anywhere else in North America. In rural areas, coyotes are often used for target practice. But the more coyotes are killed off, the more their prey flourish. The more gophers, mice, and rats flourish, the more this abundance of food stimulates whelping among the coyotes, and back they come. The more their habitat is destroyed, the more they tend to relocate to wilderness areas or just change farming districts. They also hunker down on the fringes of small towns, and, most spectacularly, like the Beverly Hillbillies, some move to the city.

In cities where the urban coyote populations are well established, if a coyote is killed, another will come to occupy its territory. It's almost as though the coyotes have a waiting list. They can be found in great quantities in Mexico, in every state of the Union except Hawaii, and in every province and territory in Canada, including the Far North.

I frequently thumb through my copy of James Halfpenny's *Scats and Tracks of North America* (2008) to help me identify the critters among which I do my hiking. When I turn to the coyote section of Halfpenny's book, I note that adults range from twenty to twenty-five pounds. I have indeed seen coyotes on the prairies and up north in that range, but I've also seen much larger ones. A quick perusal of Ian Sheldon and Tamara Hartson's *Animal Tracks of British Columbia*, confirms my suspicions. The mature coyote's weight is recorded at twenty to fifty pounds (nine to twenty-three kilograms). Although, as an ardent scatologist, I grumble about Sheldon and Hartson's exclusion of animal scat from their guidebook, I agree with their wider view on the size of coyotes.

Eastern coyotes are larger than their western counterparts. Occasionally, the eastern ones will weigh as much as fifty-five pounds. The speculation is that, for centuries, considerable cross-breeding has occurred between eastern timber wolves and eastern coyotes. When wolves were down to low populations in their habitats, they sometimes bred with coyotes. This theory explains both why eastern coyotes are larger and why they carry wolf genes.

It might also be the reason that at least some eastern coyotes tend to call out in a lower vocal range than the coyotes out west. To me, they sound somewhat like wolves. A wolf howls soulfully, like a bassoonist unlucky in love. When western coyotes gather at night, they frequently yip and squeal discordantly, like children trying out their clarinets and flutes for the first time. If a coyote had a favourite instrument, it would be called a cacophone. I've heard their eerie concerts many a time on wilderness camping trips, from Western Montana to Southern Alberta, to the Northern Rockies to Southern and Northern Saskatchewan. They can howl by themselves, howl in groups, yip-howl in groups, bark like dogs, bark and howl in combinations, woof, whine, woo-oo-wow, yelp, growl, whoop, yodel, and huff. The huffing is done by expelling air from both mouth and snout in close company with other coyotes. This might happen, for example, if some coyotes bring down an animal and the pack starts squabbling over the kill. To say the least, it is a creepy sound.

In the early fall of 2010, Kever and I did a canoe trip along the South Saskatchewan River, north of Saskatoon, with our friends Peter Nash and Linda Hearth. On our second day, we pulled in at the storied Métis community of Batoche.

We were unpacking our tents when a friendly sheep rancher came over for a chat.

The talk turned to local wildlife and eventually to coyote predation. In his first year of sheep ranching here, the man told us, he lost almost his entire flock to coyotes. He did some research and acquired a couple of Great Pyrenees-Akita mix dogs to protect his new flock. The dogs were so effective that he scarcely lost another sheep.

We pitched our two tents in a lovely glade just up from the river and just down from the site of Gabriel Dumont and Louis Riel's last stand. I was happily snoring when, from the bushes nearby, there came a maniacal chorus of yipping that made me sit up in my sleeping bag. It sounded like twenty voices or more—unhinged, dissonant notes like a woodwind section without a conductor. The yipping and yelping went on for perhaps several minutes and then shuddered huffingly to a halt. I worked myself back into my sleeping bag and fell into a light doze.

I can't remember how much time passed, but Kever and I were both awakened in the dark to a new recital, an explosion of many more voices ululating from across the river. It is not difficult to distinguish between the sound of a small chamber choir and a great big one. By that token, this gathering from across the river was the coyote equivalent of a choral assembly for Beethoven's Ninth. Their countless voices yip-yip-yipped and wailed, in wave after wave, and the smaller pack of coyotes from the nearby bushes on our side of the river tried to answer them. But the great chorus from across the river drowned them out with each reply. An indecipherable dialogue, but still a dialogue. Their singing was beyond alarming; it was awe-inspiring.

Coyote specialists have discovered that two coyotes can sound like a large family group. They direct their cries at rock walls, barns, or riverbanks to increase the echo. So this concert we were treated to on both sides of the river may have sounded as numerous as the Mormon Tabernacle Choir, but it may have come from mere dozens of animals.

❧

Fatal attacks by coyotes on humans are so rare that only two have been recorded in the past six decades, one in Canada and one in the United States. The first of these fatalities was an attack by an urban coyote in Glendale, California. In the summer of 1981, a three-year-old child was playing on her parents' driveway when a coyote dragged her away and killed her. In the fall of 2009, Taylor Mitchell, a nineteen-year-old singer-songwriter from Toronto, was doing a hike on the Skyline Trail in Cape Breton National Park (Nova Scotia) when she was attacked and killed by coyotes. She was the only person ever to die from a coyote attack in Canada.

On the other side of this sad ledger, well over four hundred thousand coyotes per year are killed in North America. They are killed by poisoning, by snares, by farmers with rifles, and by government men in helicopters. Coyote-killing contests throughout the United States claim who knows how many more animals. Their bodies are piled up for public viewing all over the country. The people responsible seem to have forgotten how successful coyotes are at killing gophers and (yes) grasshoppers. Sometimes people kill coyotes because they fear them, but this fear, however widespread it might be, bewilders me.

In Canada, during an average year, five or six people are scratched or bitten by coyotes. Recent coyote attacks in Vancouver's Stanley Park have resulted in trails being closed. In less than two months, fifteen people were chased or bitten. The main problem causing these attacks is that people in the park feed the coyotes on a regular basis.

If coyotes are allowed to live like coyotes, and hunt and feed like coyotes, they are much less likely to become a problem for tourists. They are less likely to view people as a source of food. In Vancouver, including Stanley Park of course, coyotes keep the numbers down on several species of concern: rodents, rabbits, urban deer, and non-migratory Canada geese. They also ride herd on feral cats, keeping them out of the wild spaces where they used to prey on songbirds.

Statistics tell us that domestic dogs are considerably more dangerous than wolves and coyotes put together. In the United States, pet dog attacks on humans have caused an average of thirty-one deaths per year. The moral of the story is clear: tramp through the woods and over the trails all you want, but be gentle and kind to Lassie and Rover. Feed them well.

In my neighbourhood over the past decade, the numbers of snowshoe hares have increased impressively. And now the coyotes are starting to appear. I expect that the numbers of snowshoe hares will not get out of hand here, as they have in other cities, as long as the coyotes do their job.

CHAPTER 12

Going Forth to Multiply

*S*nap quiz, name this animal: Opportunistic feeder. Mainly herbivorous. Garbage eater. Occasionally preys on wild fawns, domestic livestock such as sheep, goats, and cows. Dangerous when threatened or injured. Occasionally attacks humans but rarely kills anyone. Eyesight uncertain but has a great nose for food. Loves nuts and grain. Very hard on farmers.

If your answer is the black bear (*Ursus americanus*), you would not be far off the mark. But if I told you that this particular beast is an ungulate (an animal with hooves), that it is featured lovingly in cartoons, feel-good films, and children's books, you might be tempted to cry out "pig!"

Bingo.

I'm talking here about wild pigs or, as some prefer to say, feral hogs. Pigs arrived in the West Indies on Columbus's ships in 1492, but they came to North America proper in the early sixteenth century with the arrival of Hernando de Soto in Florida. As the incursions from Spain and Western Europe increased, more and more ships arrived in North America carrying domestic pigs to provide the invaders with fresh meat. The pigs were good at finding their own food, so they were low maintenance and inexpensive. When the Spaniards marched inland, the remaining settlers often left their pigs untended to fend for themselves, and some of these became the first wild pigs—as things turned out, very wild. From Florida, they foraged and rooted their way north and westward. After the Spanish incursion, more European settlers arrived—and more pigs. The new settlers also allowed their pigs to range freely. Many more of these animals went off into the bush and joined the herds that came before them. America's first libertarians, one might say.

Much later, a Eurasian strain of pig, usually referred to as wild boar, was introduced from Europe to be hunted by sportsmen. These imports began arriving in the early twentieth century. Many were deliberately released into the wild and many more escaped their handlers. The early strains of domestic pigs-turned-feral and the wild boars that came centuries later are closely related cousins—like Rocky Mountain grizzlies and brown bears, but much more of a problem than bears. What we usually call wild boars came straight from the wild in European forests.

On the other hand, the collared peccaries (*Pecari tajacu*) found in desert scrub regions of Mexico and in the American Southwest have escaped the widespread infamy of their larger wild pig cousins, possibly because peccaries are considered a native species. These smaller herbivores came north more than thirty million years ago from the jungles and woodlands of South and Central America. They are less predacious in all senses of the word than feral hogs; less prolific, less destructive, and not at all dangerous to people. (I think they're kind of adorable.)

But the imported pigs-gone-wild known as *Sus scrofa* are something else. These animals average around two hundred pounds and sometimes attain a weight of five hundred pounds (almost two hundred and thirty kilograms) or more. They are amazingly fertile animals. Males begin to breed as early as twelve months, and sows at around eight months. They average 1.2 litters a year, with four to six piglets to a litter. They have the highest reproductive rate of any of the ungulates. In 1982, it was estimated that the feral hog population in the lower forty-eight states had swollen to around two million, four hundred thousand. In 2016, the estimate rose to almost seven million.

Wild pigs eat such a wide variety of flora and fauna that the list of what they *don't* eat may be rather short. The following menu of wild pig preferences is by no means comprehensive: beech, oak, and chestnut mast; rhizomes, roots, forbs, flowering plants, and bulbs; leaves and branches; countless invertebrates such as insects, spiders, crustaceans, snails, and slugs; worms and leeches; young goats, calves, and lambs; whitetail deer fawns, rabbits and carrion; animal scat; reptiles and amphibians; ground-nesting birds and their eggs; and sometimes massive amounts of watermelons, cantaloupes, peanuts, potatoes, corn, soybeans, rice, oats, rye, sorghum, and wheat.

The state of Texas has not exactly cornered the market on feral hogs, but they are off to a disconcertingly good start with roughly three million of them. The other four to five million feral hogs can be found in thirty-five other states, including Hawaii. They have been more recently established in various regions of Canada, as well.

The considerable damage the feral hogs inflict on wilderness habitats and farms, with their burrowing ways, is a fast-growing problem. In Texas alone, the annual damage comes to US$120 million, mainly from increasingly large pig herds rooting, trampling, wallowing, milling around, and consuming standing grain, hay, and orchard fruits. In sensitive ecological areas and farm country, they foul creeks and marshes with fecal matter. To be fair to these wild porkers, their status as creek foulers and marsh poopers pales in comparison with the pollution caused by the corporate pig farms in the Carolinas reported on not many years ago. But that is grist for another mill.

Again, just in Texas, the cost of motor vehicle collisions involving feral hogs is currently approaching US$40 million annually. Another concern, in the United States and Canada, are the bacterial, fungal, and viral diseases, including African swine fever, which the wild pigs can pass on to domestic livestock. The overall cost in dealing with the ravages of wild pigs in the United States is about US$2.1 billion annually. Altogether, these figures constitute a strong indictment of wild pigs as the second most destructive animal in North America. Human beings are still securely in first place.

Early Sunday morning, November 24, 2019. Chambers County, Texas. An eighty-four-year-old man glanced out the window of his rural home in Anahuac, Texas, about an hour's drive east of Houston. He could plainly see the white sedan of Christine Rollins parked by his front door, but why had she not come inside? He had heard his dogs barking but there was no evidence of trespassers. For more than a year, Ms. Rollins's job had been taking care of the old man and his wife, and she had never showed up late. Ms. Rollins was a cheerful, kindly soul. The old couple had found her to be indispensable in helping them to maintain their lives in the country.

It was still a secret, but the old man and his wife were part of a conspiracy to throw her a party on Christmas Day for her sixtieth birthday.

The old man eased himself down the front steps and out into his yard, which fronted on Highway 61. He spotted something on a small patch of grass that did not seem to belong there. He trudged closer, stopped, and stared.

After a forensic investigation by the sheriff's department, and after the autopsy, a medical examiner announced that Christine Rollins had been attacked and killed by a herd of feral hogs. She had indeed arrived on time that morning for her shift with the old couple. She parked close to the front door, got out of the car, locked it, and started for the house. It was only a few steps, but she never made it. Perhaps the sound of her vehicle had disturbed the pigs. How many, no one knows, but they had probably been bedded down in the cool shadows next to the house.

To remain cool, wild pigs usually travel and forage in the dark and in the shadows. Like wild deer, they remain hidden in forested areas and bushes, and feed mostly at night.

Christine's was the first death caused by feral hogs in Texas since 1996, and the fifth such recorded death due to feral hogs in recent American history.

Much of what I have come across in my research about wild pigs comes with a whiff of anti-porcine propaganda—let's say a well-earned resentment. But their feeding raids and clashes with humans seem to me more inevitable than willful. If I compare the attacks by feral hogs to the recent increase in attacks by bears and cougars, there is one obvious trend in common: the surge of human population, and their encroachment upon rural terrain. This population shift reveals itself in the swarms of resorts, theme parks, recreation areas, suburbs, exurbs, acreages, and hobby farms. There are fewer hunters in most of these places, but many more hikers, birders, nature lovers, and of course non-hunting gun owners.

As is the case with bears and cougars, attacks on humans by wild pigs are quite rare. A study was made by David Wilson of 412 reported attacks by wild pigs on a total of 665 humans in the United States from 1825 to 2012. The disparity in numbers between attacks and people is because some of these attacks were launched against groups of people. The study includes four of the five people who died from such attacks. (Christine Rollins's tragic death happened six years after this study.) The 412 attacks by feral hogs average out to be a little more than two attacks per year—many of which were scary but bloodless: people being chased or treed by wild pigs. Three of the four fatalities listed were hunters killed by wounded pigs.

This is my way of saying that, although it behooves us all to be careful in the vicinity of wild pigs, being attacked by them is an extreme rarity. For me, the only disquieting statistic in the Jack Mayer (2013) study is that seventy per cent of the 412 attacks happened during the last twelve years of the 187-year survey. This is not surprising, of course, when we look at the recent population explosion of wild pigs and the expansion of people living in suburbs and acreages.

The measures to control herds of feral hogs include hunting them as recreation as we do with other wild animals, bounty hunting, hunting with tracking dogs, night hunting, shooting them from small aircraft, and trapping them in various ways. Unlike capturing nuisance bears and fly-fishing for trout, there is no catch and release for wild pigs.

The least successful approaches for cutting down on the population of wild pigs are recreational and trophy hunting. Recreational hunting often involves catching and transporting pigs all over the United States to wilderness areas and game farms. Not surprisingly, this helps to increase feral hog populations. Shooting big boars for trophies also has little effect on population. Going after sows and juveniles does have an impact on population. Depending on whether the pigs are in heavy bush or open fields, night shooting with silenced rifles has a greater impact on populations. Shooting wild pigs from a variety of small aircraft can also be effective, if, as in the case of night shooting, there are lots of pigs in farmers' fields and other wide open spaces.

But a more effective method of population control has evolved in recent years: catching wild pigs in baited corral traps and then killing them. These spacious traps can be monitored and triggered remotely using phones or laptops. I imagine that a large enough corral trap, assembled in the right place, could capture an entire herd in a relatively short period of time.

I am slightly appalled by the information I have set forth here, because the last thing I want to do with this book is encourage gun-happy men to kill wild animals that are more and more scarce and vulnerable. But wild pigs are anything but scarce and vulnerable in North America, and, as I have indicated, they do a surprising amount of damage.

In the forests of the Transylvanian and Carpathian Mountains in Eastern Romania, wild boars have flourished for centuries, but their populations have been controlled by wild predators such as wolves and lynxes. In my own province of Saskatchewan, especially in the eastern parklands and prairies, we have a very sparse population of wolves and an even sparser population of cougars. So there are very few natural checks on our burgeoning herds of wild pigs that root their way through farms and wild spaces. Even with the efforts of skilled marksmen, there seems to be no way of controlling *Sus scrofa*. Unless we devise local methods to control them, the moveable feast that is their lives will continue to grow.

Feral Hog

CHAPTER 13

Heeding the Wolf

I missed that night's chorus but now open the window a crack when
I go to bed. Yes, even in winter. I'm hoping to hear the wolf's song.
I want the cascade of notes to send shivers up my spine and touch
my soul. I want to hear the wolves but I don't want them to come
too close. For their safety, not mine.
—Return of the Wolf, PAULA WILD

*T*he winter of 2006–07 in Saskatchewan came too early for many a
farmer. The storms around the towns of Humboldt and Muenster in
East Central Saskatchewan were particularly brutal. On the grounds
of St. Peter's Abbey, there is a field adjacent to the monastery that
was used to grow an experimental strain of organic Marquis wheat.
When the first of the blizzards descended in mid-October, the crop
was not ready for harvest, so by the end of the month it lay beneath

an impressive blanket of snow. Most of the crop was flattened, but some of the stalks of wheat near windbreaks poked bravely above the drifts.

As the wind shrieked across the prairie and through the copses where starving deer were bedded, they must have picked up the scent of all that unharvested wheat. From November to January, like pilgrims seeking absolution, the deer ventured into the trees and the grounds of St. Peter's Abbey, forming a sizeable herd. In the evening around the time of vespers, when the monks had left the chapel and the monastery had gone still, about one hundred whitetails could be seen moving from the protection of the Abbey's orchard into the field of wheat.

Kever and I arrived at St. Peter's Monastery in early February for a writers' and artists' retreat, she to do some painting and I to work on fiction. We were able to drive there safely by traveling between two blizzards. We couldn't wait to get down to work and to build a quinzhee in our off hours. A quinzhee is a structure made of snow, built to house from one to a dozen people, depending on the occasion. At St. Pete's, the writers and artists show up in shifts to shovel a seven-foot pile, and then hollow it out from the inside to create a cozy little space in the top half of the structure. We light candles and gather there on cold nights.

That first night, Kever and I settled into a room in the guest wing overlooking a tall windbreak that stood between us and the doomed field of wheat. Just before bedtime, Kever opened our window enough to let in some cool air, and soon after that, just as I was closing my eyes, I heard a low and mournful howl. It seemed to come from the trees close to our open window. The animal howled again. From somewhere off in the night, in response to the howling, came a wild chorus of yipping.

ఆ

Breakfasts at St. Peter's Abbey, among the writers, artists, monks and kitchen staff, are very jovial. The Guestmaster, Father Demetrius, greeted us with his customary repertoire of good cheer and gleeful sarcasm. I asked him about the previous night's performance outside our bedroom window.

"Does someone around here own a husky?"

"No," said Demetrius with a wicked smile, "that was our wolf."

A wolf on the prairie. And a pack of coyotes. And perhaps some kind of a connection between these two traditional enemies. Before I could form a question about all this, Demetrius smiled and added, "He's eating rather well these days."

After work, in mid-to-late afternoon when the weather had cleared, a group of us strapped on our snowshoes and skis and went exploring for signs of wolf predation. Father Demetrius had given us some clues as to where we might begin our search: check out the bushy fringes on the near side of the wheat field.

Five or six of us trudged over to the nearest fringe of trees and bushes that lay beyond Kever's and my bedroom window. Immediately I spied a scattering of blood, bones, and deer hide in the snow. I could tell it was a fresh kill because the remains of the deer were not covered over by yesterday's blizzard. The meat had been gnawed from the rib cages. The deer's stomach, stuffed with browse from the previous night's feeding, had been torn out and set aside. Here and there around the skeleton were some large paw prints and dozens of small ones. I was drawn to one of the smaller prints that lay on top of one of the big ones. There were a number of these doubled prints, which suggested to me that the coyotes had come to feed off the scraps after the departure of the wolf. But that howling from the previous night, followed by the chorus of yipping—what was that all about? Were the coyotes in league with the wolf? Did the wolf rely on the coyotes to send the deer his way? Did the wolf willingly share his kill with the coyotes? Did their duet constitute some sort of tactical dialogue?

In his walks around the wheat field, Father Demetrius had located thirteen kill sites, whitetail remains buried under layers of snow. With the driving snow, these kill sites had formed mounds. In about an hour of tramping and gliding, our group found seven of the kill sites. Regardless of when or how these deer were brought down, the kill sites had similarities. The stomachs and their contents had in most cases been ripped out and discarded. Whenever we were able to see paw prints, there would be a few huge ones and many small ones. Again, I wondered if this was an example of co-operative hunting between the two species.

I began to ask questions of the people who lived at or near the Abbey. I found five people who had seen the wolf over the course of the winter. They referred to it as either the dark wolf or the black wolf. Father Demetrius was one of them. One day in January, he and his colleague, Father Paul, were driving west towards Humboldt when they spotted several deer running through deep snow towards the highway. They were pursued by a dark-coloured wolf, and the wolf was gaining on them. A wolf's paws are nicely adapted to running on packed snow. When the paws hit the snow, they spread out. Deer have small hooves that plunge through the snow, making them struggle. But these frantic deer managed to maintain enough speed to make it to the highway. They scampered across and left the wolf behind. It was a narrow escape.

Another person I interviewed, an editor for the Abbey's press, had spotted two wolves northeast of St. Pete's the previous fall, presumably our dark male with a light grey female. The editor assumed that they were a mated pair of gray wolves (timber wolves, he called them), and someone had told him, later that same fall, that the female had been killed by an automobile. There were no reports of dens or cubs.

On skis one sunny morning, I followed some fresh tracks that went parallel to the highway towards the nearby town of Muenster. The tracks had come out of the forest that grew on the south side of the railway, less than one kilometre north of the Abbey. These tracks were not accompanied by any human ones, and they were big, like husky tracks. I assumed they belonged to our wolf. There had been another snowfall during the night. Because the tracks were so fresh, I assumed they must have been made in the pre-dawn hours. About twenty metres from the wolf tracks was a fresh set of multiple coyote tracks, perhaps half a dozen animals, also heading in the direction of town. The coyotes had kept their distance from the lone wolf. It was hard to resist the assumption that they were following the wolf and doing so at a safe distance.

A bunch of us had built our quinzhee in some deep snow, big enough for seven or eight writers and artists to fit in. It was back in the woods where only we could locate it, a beautiful rounded structure seven feet high and much wider at the base, a house of snow in the shape of an igloo. On one of the last nights of the retreat a few of us thought it would be nice to gather by candlelight in the quinzhee, read a few poems and say our goodbyes. When it was dark and we were gathered in the common room, we hesitated. It was cold outside and we were cozy inside, but I don't think that was the only reason. Our problem had to do with the wolf. Why had we never seen it in all our wanderings through the orchard and the woods? Probably because it was a nocturnal predator. Could it have been denning in our quinzhee? Just a wild guess, but it was enough to make me, and all the other retreating artists, choose to remain safely in the common room until bedtime. Later that night, Father Demetrius took a walk northeast of the monks' residence along a monastery laneway that led to a grid road. Ahead of him, and also to his left, lay a windbreak of planted spruce, black beneath a bright moon. Behind him and to his right the deer would have gathered for their nightly feed. Demetrius stopped to light a cigarette, and when he looked up, the black wolf was observing him. On the moon-lit snow, it stood out clearly. Behind the wolf, not close enough to risk being attacked, a pack of coyotes was also scrutinizing Father Demetrius. He paused for a moment, then perhaps realized that he was standing between the animals and their meal. He turned and walked back to his residence.

Father Demetrius's sighting of the wolf and coyotes demonstrated to me the uneasy relationship between the two predatory species. The scene was not a symbiotic gathering between wolf and coyotes, because only the coyotes would have benefited from the wolf's presence. The choruses we heard over many nights between wolf and coyotes may have been closer to sabre-rattling than co-operative chatter between two predatory species.

We used to call them timber wolves but now we call them gray wolves. Under the right conditions, including the presence of a healthy number of large prey animals (deer, elk, moose, caribou, buffalo), gray wolves (*Canis lupus*) can reach a weight of 145 pounds (66 kilograms). Some sources give heavier estimates, but these were likely gray wolves with full stomachs. There are reports of larger subspecies, such as the Yukon (or Alaskan) wolf and the Eurasian wolf, but the gray wolves that inhabit the forests of the Canadian West, the Canadian North, Alaska, and scattered habitats in the lower forty-eight states, are considered the dominant wolf species on our continent.

Owing to some impressive research in recent years, we know considerably more about wolves than we did in the twentieth century. For example, we know that there may be as many as three hundred thousand wolves around the world. There are as many as sixty thousand wolves in Canada and another sixteen thousand in the United States. Roughly nine thousand of the American wolves live in Alaska, and the rest are scattered across the Midwest and the mountain states. Minnesota has by far the biggest population in the lower forty-eight states, about two thousand, seven hundred wolves—a number that I find heartening. Until recently, Wisconsin could boast more than one thousand animals, but that was before a recent slaughter of two hundred and sixteen wolves during their breeding season, mostly by licensed hunters.

We know much about wolves' mating practices, how they care for their young, how they hunt individually and communally, how their territories shift with the size of their packs, how the male and female alphas organize and lead their packs, and how they train the pups to hunt. Rick McIntyre, a naturalist and wolf specialist, is a conduit for such information. He has been observing wolves for decades, and compiling field notes on the various packs that have flourished in the Yellowstone ecosystem since their introduction in 1995 and 1996. Until I read McIntyre's two recent books, *The Rise of Wolf* 8 (2019) and *The Reign of Wolf* 21 (2020), I knew little about wolves' domestic lives. But through McIntyre's field notes, I learned, for example, about how wolf packs nurture and care for their pups. Throughout their first ten weeks or so, they are cared for and guarded by any number of cub-sitters, including, at times, their original mothers. After a month or more in the den, the pups are weaned and they begin their explorations. The switch from mother's milk to meat happens once the pups are moved to a nesting area, a rendezvous point above ground. The hunting wolves, male and female, come back from their latest kill, gorged with meat, and when the hungry pups come out to greet them, they regurgitate their offerings for the cubs to devour.

I've also been rereading Ian McAllister's book, *The Last Wild Wolves* (2007), which preceded McIntyre's two volumes by more than a decade. McAllister and his crew focused their attentions on the wolves of the Great Bear Rainforest along British Columbia's northern coast. McAllister risked much to get close to the wolves—in a sense, joining and rejoining the pack with each visit. To manage this, McAllister built up an unusual amount of trust between himself and his four-legged friends. He has much to say about their foraging for food and their unusual diets. These wolves feed not only on ungulates, but also on salmon, harbour seals, sea lions, beached whales, Canada geese, shellfish, black bears, and even the occasional giant squid.

Unlike cougars, who are extremely reclusive, wolves can be observed by a variety of people under the right circumstances, something I learned in Douglas Smith and Gary Ferguson's book, *The Decade of the Wolf: Returning the Wild to Yellowstone* (2012). The much-publicized gray wolves of the greater Yellowstone region in Wyoming came originally from Alberta and British Columbia in a 1995-96 reintroduction program. The initial success of this transplanting of thirty-one Canadian wolves brought legions of ecotourists to the park, an ongoing lupus love-in. I watched them one summer, gathered like birders by the side of the road. These wolf enthusiasts were surprisingly knowledgeable about the different packs. They knew the players, and they had read the latest updates on the size of each pack. They gathered to relate stories about their favourite wolves. Like football fans scrutinizing the rosters, these people were eager for each day's game to begin.

This great awareness of and love for wolves is evident all through Paula Wild's *Return of the Wolf: Conflict and Coexistence* (2018), in which the author steeps herself in the history of human interaction with wolves, from the ancient myths (from Japan, Russia, Scandinavia, India and many other countries) to the Indigenous narratives of the Americas. To write her book, she had to become a wolf scholar.

I found similar erudition and love for wolves among members of the burgeoning eco and anthrozoologist communities in North America. G.A. Bradshaw's *Carnivore Minds* (2017) and Richard Louv's *Our Wild Calling* (2019) come readily to mind. I am increasingly aware that these writers and their animal-bonding followers are like distant cousins to me. If this community, centred on human–animal relationships, were a church, I would be a member in good standing. We are mostly city dwellers whose heart is in the country. Perhaps one of our patron saints, along with Henry David Thoreau and Aldo Leopold, would be Farley Mowat, who published *Never Cry Wolf* in 1963. Both Thoreau and Mowat told some real stretchers, but surely in a good cause.

Okay, let's not get carried away here. The last of many books and articles that I read in preparation for this account was a recent publication by Harold Johnson, *Cry Wolf: Inquest into the True Nature of a Predator* (2020). Fairly or not, for the purpose of discussion, he divides up the world of wolf watchers into "romantics" and "gun people." The romantics (like me) want to place the wolf in an elevated category—wise, majestic, and soulful. The romantics lean rather heavily on the concept of wolf as sacred spirit. Just as wilderness land is sacred to us, so must the wolf be sacred. I have probably uttered things like this without much thinking about them. Harold Johnson would no doubt spot this in me and my fellow wolf lovers from a mile away.

Harold Johnson. He passed away in February 2022, but people still talk about him in the present tense. Aside from having been a brawler, athlete, miner, graduate of Harvard's law school, lawyer, prosecutor, and writer, Harold Johnson descended from Cree trappers and had his own trapline. He was once stalked and threatened by a wolf—a narrow escape. At times he had been fearful of wolves in his northern region. Johnson was also steeped in the spiritual traditions and stories of the Cree in Northern Saskatchewan, so he looked hard at the romantics' hierarchical notions that exalt the noble wolf above other animals in creation. Our worries over the survival of endangered wolves are "well founded," he tells us, because wolves have been senselessly slaughtered for centuries.

However, Johnson reminds wolf romantics that we have failed to put our sentiments into context. In the natural world, Johnson's people believe that all nature's creatures are potential "spirit helpers." And majestic, intelligent, strong and agile though the wolf is, it is no more special than the woodpecker. "Even plants," Johnson argues, "can be a familiar to an animist" (*Cry Wolf*).

The gun people, as opposed to the romantics, see themselves as pragmatic. The wolf is dangerous. It kills pets and calves, and could attack human beings. The gun people want bounties on various carnivores to assist them in their ongoing heroic battle. A few years before Johnson wrote his book, a gun lobby in Saskatchewan approached the provincial government for a bounty on coyotes. According to them, coyotes were apparently out of control and killing livestock. If coyotes were allowed to keep propagating, they would get mange, which would make them suffer. (No examples of mange were in evidence.) But the lobbyists got their bounty on coyotes and no doubt the government got the shooters' votes. They slaughtered thousands of coyotes and then were dismayed to find a big increase in gopher populations. (Hmmm. Wonder why.) So they agitated for a bounty on gophers.

"The truth," Johnson tells us, is "that gun people want an excuse to shoot their guns" because shooting wolves, coyotes, and gophers is "exciting to them." Lost among this zeal to kill anything in the woods that is big and ferocious is the simple fact that almost no one in North America has been killed by a wolf in the past century. There have been a few exceptions in cases of captive or rabid wolves, but human mortality from wild healthy wolves and coyotes is extremely rare.

Johnson's book was a response to the investigation of the death in Northern Saskatchewan of a likeable and promising young man from Ontario, Kenton Carnegie, in 2005. That winter, Carnegie went walking alone through the snow and didn't return for supper to his work camp. It is almost certain that wolves took him down and partially consumed his body. Around this camp, wolves had become habituated to humans and the food they'd been throwing into their unfenced garbage dump. There had been a number of wolf problems around other northern mining camps as well, but this incident, where Carnegie was working, happened at the camp at Points North. As it happens, I was in Points North to go fishing five years before Carnegie's death. At that time, Points North was a hub for bush pilots and eager anglers from the south. From there, anglers would board smaller planes and head for fishing lodges. Points North was the gateway to good fishing. In 2005, it became briefly infamous for dangerous wolf packs.

Five years after the death of Kenton Carnegie, Candice Berner, a teacher in Chignik, Alaska, was also, very likely, killed by wolves. I mention these two tragic incidents to remind readers that wolves, like coyotes and wild pigs, are occasionally dangerous. Every living creature on earth, Harold Johnson has argued, "has three commandments: eat, don't be eaten, and procreate." A hungry wolf who has come to associate humans with food, and who has not learned from its elders to fear humans, will occasionally cross that fatal line. But learning from its elders is difficult if the alpha wolves are getting shot.

I pass on these cautions in the spirit of Herman Melville, who warns we romantics (dreamers, transcendentalists, platonists, and pantheists alike), who gaze out, as it were, from the masthead to the hypnotic ocean: "While this sleep, this dream is on ye, move your foot or hand an inch; slip your hold at all; and your identity comes back in horror. Over Descartian vortices you hover. And perhaps, at midday, in the fairest weather, with one half-throttled shriek you drop through that transparent air into the summer sea, no more to rise for ever. Heed it well, ye Pantheists!" (*Moby Dick*, 1851).

☙

The first wolf that really caught my attention was at the Forestry Farm Zoo in Saskatoon. On a few occasions, I would signal to the largest wolf in the enclosure to follow me as I galloped past the fence, and he would run beside me on his side no more than five feet away. I acquired an affection for the old wolf, and it was great fun to run with him. But I was never sure if this game was a case of a bored animal communing with a kindred human, or a bored predator chasing an annoying tourist. Heed it well, ye Pantheists.

I was fifty-five years old when I saw my first wolf in the wild. This happened up north near Big River, Saskatchewan: a very large, dirty-white animal lying in a sunny clearing above the road. When Kever turned the car around for a better view, the wolf rose on long legs to its full height, turned slowly away and drifted into the trees. Its whiteness was less impressive than its great size.

That was in 1996. I've seen many more since then. One of my favourite wolf encounters happened in Narrow Hills Provincial Park, a short drive south of Little Bear Lake. I was driving with Kever and my Toronto nephew, Nick Carpenter. It was a rainy day with a chill in the air. We were on a gravel road a few miles from the highway when we spotted a Canada goose flying up from a ditch filled with water. Instead of veering away from our vehicle, the goose flapped right past my window in a panic. The source of its alarm was a wet wolf standing on the road. We slowed down and the wolf crossed the road, leapt over the ditch and climbed up to the edge of the woods. It turned about and glared down at us. How do we know when a wolf is angry at us? The animal doesn't have to growl or show its teeth. We can sense the snarly attitude, which translates roughly as, *You have just cost me a meal.*

Perhaps my recent wolf sightings signal a larger presence of wolves in the southernmost reach of the boreal forest, into the parkland, and even on the prairies. Hundreds of moose have descended from the north into the central and southern Saskatchewan farmlands. With fewer people living permanently on farms, deer populations have increased in recent years. It may be that the wolves are descending from the northern forests to follow their prey. In the winter of 2010, I scared up a wolf at Beaver Creek, about twenty kilometres south of Saskatoon. Early in the winter of 2021, a small wolf pack was sighted about twenty-five kilometres west of Saskatoon.

During the past decade, wolves have been observed throughout the prairies and parklands of South and Central Saskatchewan. A partial list of sightings, dead and alive, would include the vicinities of Glaslyn, Naicam, Yorkton, Saskatoon, Swift Current, Lloydminster, the Battlefords, Moose Jaw, Leader, Sceptre, Cabri, Tompkins, Cypress Hills, Moose Mountain Provincial Park, and Duck Mountain Provincial Park.

Many of these transient wolves were sighted, or shot, in the Qu'Appelle and Saskatchewan River systems. Some of the sightings may have been large coyotes mistaken for wolves. Perhaps some of those spotted on the prairies were ephemeral wolves, young unmated males that left their packs to find new territory.

They are certainly showing up on the prairies. It is possible that wolves are drawn to farming country nowadays because fewer farmers live on the land. This might also partly explain why cougars have been seen in isolated pockets of South and Central Saskatchewan. This geographical shift worries me, because, like the migrating moose, the wolves and cougars make inviting targets for eager shooters.

Since the early days of settlement there have been many wolf haters and heedless wolf killers. Wolfers hunt them on horseback. Trappers covet their furs. Farmers and ranchers poison them with strychnine. Airborne marksmen shoot them from small planes and helicopters. Snowmobilers run them down, exhaust them, and shoot them. Armed men kill them simply because they are afraid of wolves. Wealthy trophy hunters a long way from wolf habitat fly in to hunting camps, bag a wolf, and fly out.

Some of the wolf killings are understandable, because, let's face it, wolves occasionally dine on cattle, sheep, chickens, and other farm animals. The loss of one or two calves can send a small operation into the red. Sometimes northern subsistence hunters find themselves competing with the wolves for declining herds of caribou. My greatest sympathy is still with the wolf lovers, however sentimental their perceptions might be.

An accepted argument for protecting and bringing back wolves to their original habitats has much to do with what scientists call trophic cascades. Like cougars, wolves are apex predators, meaning that they sit at the top of the food chain. Trophic cascades begin with the impact of sunlight on the region's flora, fueling the food chain for the ungulates that feed on grass and other plants. These hoofed animals (goats, moose, deer, elk) are killed and consumed by wolves, cougars, and other carnivores, and their remains are consumed by carrion eaters (vultures, ravens, crows, magpies, and bugs). This chain of growth and predation allows the powerful rays of the sun to drive the cycle through the entire ecosystem. The wolves and their competitors (bears and cougars) at the top of the food chain can also have a huge and positive influence on the life around them. Not only do they prevent the ungulates from overgrazing, but in doing so, they restore the plants, which host the insects, which bring back the birdlife. I'll stop here, because the interconnections are so rich and complex that I can't begin to account for them all.

In summary: kill off the wolves, and the ungulates will over-graze their browse—willows, aspens, cottonwoods, moss, and other plants. Bring back the wolves, and in certain vulnerable ecosystems, the plants regenerate and the fauna will follow. This is the beauty of the trophic cascade.

Bring back the ecosystem and the scientists will follow. Competing teams of scientists have been studying the indirect effects of this burgeoning population of wolves on the ecosystem. But (not to repeat myself), kill off the apex carnivores and the forest will fade away.

In the early autumn of my life, I have been blessed by wolves. If memory serves, I have seen twenty-two more wolves since that day of the white wolf near Big River in 1996. I don't include those instances where wolves howled unseen in the nearby bush, and I don't include the sightings that could not be confirmed. I have spot-ted wolves in Northern Ontario, south of Kenora; in Alberta, east of

Jasper; and in Wyoming's Yellowstone Park. By far, however, most of my sightings have been in Northern Saskatchewan. Each sighting has been memorable for me, but the most memorable experience of all was the black wolf of St. Peter's Abbey—the one we never saw.

Gray Wolf

CHAPTER 14

The Cat Came Back

*You come out and the animals will find you, even if you never
know they are there. Whether you are observant, curious, unaware,
reluctant, or apathetic, they will find you. As they move around
you, they will make tracks of different sizes, different gaits, different
numbers and shapes of toes and claws, leaving signatures as they
turn their weight into the ground to watch you.*
—CRAIG CHILDS, *The Animal Dialogues*

I am twenty-one years old. I am about to start a summer job at
the Jasper National Park Fish Hatchery. It's a warm evening in early
May with the dusk coming on, and I'm returning to town after a
long walk. Below the Yellowhead Highway to my left, the Athabasca
River drifts by. To my right is a dry patch of meadow slanting up into
the trees above the road. A car is pulled over on the right shoulder,

and twenty or thirty metres up the slope, a herd of bighorn sheep grazes the sparse, arid grass. A young family sits in the car, peering uphill. The father is at the wheel with his window down, and he looks up at me.

"Show him," he says to his wife.

She passes a pair of binoculars to her husband and he hands them to me.

"There," he whispers, with some urgency. "Up above the sheep."

I train his binoculars on some animals peering intently down at the sheep. They have a stealthy look about them.

"Boy, wad you see?"

"I dunno, coyotes? Wolves?"

"Look again," he says. "You look careful."

I adjust the binoculars and direct them at the mysterious animals gathered above the bighorns. There are four or five of them, partially obscured by bush, grouped close together. Too big for coyotes and they don't look like wolves.

I gasped. "Oh my God, it's a pack of, a pack of…"

"Mountain lions," the man says. He speaks with an accent of some kind. "A whole family. Now look down. No, down there. By the falling tree."

On our side of a fallen Douglas fir, facing up and away from us, an animal crouches, staring at the sheep. This one looks bigger than the cougars further up the slope.

The man's accent is Italian. I learn that he works in Jasper for the CNR. When I hand him back his binoculars, he offers me a ride into town. I check the back seat of his car, which is filled with children, and I turn down his offer. He drives away, and as the light fades, I continue to watch the big cats on the slope. It comes to me, suddenly, that I am all alone near a bunch of cougars. Probably hungry cougars. Like a nervous elk, I hoof the couple of miles back to Jasper.

This happened in 1963, and for years I have poked away at the memory with some skepticism. An entire family of cougars? The cubs seemed almost as big as the adults, so they would have been juveniles, almost old enough to head out on their own. The large cougar closest to the car might have been the father of the litter, because males can be much larger than females. But that assumption bothers me now because I have learned that male cougars do not hang around with their families. And among cougars, there is no such thing as prides. Perhaps the lone cougar crouched next to the fallen tree seemed bigger than the ones up the slope because it was crouched closer to me.

Cougars: *Felis concolor*, mountain lions, pumas, panthers, painters. They are solitary hunters, raised from birth to be independent. Unlike wolves, cougars have no communal structure to help with the rearing of kittens. Wolf pups will grow up with both parents and cub-sitters watching over them. When the pups are old enough to eat meat, a member of their pack will bring back meat from a kill and regurgitate it into their mouths. And, in some cases, wolves might remain with their original packs for years.

When cougar kittens are about one month old, their mothers will leave them alone in their den for hours while she hunts. When the kittens are around two months old, they start following their mother on hunts. She will often leave them at a kill site for several days until she makes another kill. Instead of remaining in a family group or a pack, young cougars leave their mothers at around eighteen months, and they must carve out a territory for themselves. If a young cougar attempts to linger with its mother, the mother will often scare it off to find new ground of its own, meaning a large unclaimed stretch of wilderness with good numbers of deer, elk, moose, feral pigs, mountain sheep, or smaller prey, and with no big rival males to drive them off. A young male cougar, if he survives to adulthood, needs to grow big enough (roughly one hundred and thirty-five to one hundred and fifty pounds) to fend off rival males. Male cougars do not tolerate other cougars, except for the occasional female for mating, often in early winter. Female cougars are also solitary hunters, except when they allow their kittens, around the age of six to nine months, to hunt with them.

I used to assume that the severe strictures on kittens and juveniles, as described above, was pretty much the whole story. But with the advent of GPS technology, satellite collars, and trail cameras, improved data on cougars is now available. Recent research reveals exceptions to the loner prototype. We now have photographic evidence that cougars—even male cougars—do, on occasion, socialize in diverse groups. So what I beheld at dusk on that evening in May 1963 could have been one of those occasions when males, females, and juvenile cats gathered peacefully for the hunt. Unusual perhaps, because at other times, the males will attempt to kill off the cubs of a female in order to bring about their own genetic dynasty.

A day or two later, when I walked that slanting stretch of meadow in better light, I found no evidence of a kill. But what I had witnessed that night—a family hunting excursion or (less likely) a social occasion—was an extraordinary bit of luck for me.

During that same spring of 1963, I saw another cougar at the hatchery where I was working. I was with Willie Baillard, another hatchery labourer, and we were just arriving for work in the truck, passing through the hatchery gate. We spotted a young animal, and it was peering down at one of our spawning pools that contained big rainbows and lake trout that moved in aimless circles. Because of the hum from the pump that circulated the water, the cat didn't hear us. As we crept towards the pond for a better look, the young cougar was trying to scoop out a fish. It may have caught our scent, because suddenly it looked back our way and then took off. We chased the cat past the outdoor ponds and into the bush. It was very fast and it leapt over deadfalls like an Olympic hurdler.

Well, not quite. It's the other way around. Whether they know it or not, with every race, Olympic hurdlers try to mimic the sprinting cougar, and they do so with limited success.

People familiar with cougars will have occasion to wonder how they have managed to survive the onslaught of hunters, trappers, houndsmen, drunk drivers, and poisoners who, since the arrival of Europeans, have killed hundreds of thousands of their kind. An example of this carnage is provided by Wayne Pacelle, a cougar advocate working for the Humane Society of the United States in Washington, DC. He tells us that, between 1907 and 1978, "hunters, ranchers, and damage control agents killed at least 66,665 cougars." Until well into the twentieth century, cougars were considered to be varmints. They had been driven from over two thirds of their traditional territory in North America, which includes a vast territory in the Eastern United States and Canada.

From very early times, whitetails and mule deer, cougars' food of choice, were hunted as relentlessly as bison, and the scarcity of these ungulates exacerbated the cougars' decline. By the early twentieth century, aggressive government programs and bounties had almost eliminated the remaining cougars in the United States. A survey begun in 1963, supervised by a young scientist, Maurice Hornocker, estimated that less than six thousand, five hundred of the animals remained in his country. Around this time, laws were passed to put an end to the unrestricted hunting of deer. And so, throughout the last two or three decades of the twentieth century, a kind of ecological miracle took place: the cat came back.

Viable populations have been re-established throughout twelve of the western states: Texas, New Mexico, Nevada, Arizona, Wyoming, Colorado, Utah, Idaho, Montana, Washington, Oregon, and California. California has a human population of close to forty million people, about two million more than the entire country of Canada, but even around Los Angeles, its most populated region, cougars have returned. Recently there have been frequent sightings in Nebraska and Missouri. Minnesota and, especially, Wisconsin have more deer than they can count, and the cougars have followed. The same can be said of the Dakotas, Kansas, Oklahoma, Iowa, and Illinois. We can't go so far as to say that these midwestern states all have vibrant, re-established populations of cougars, but we can safely say that the cougars are branching out and following the river valleys into new (old) territory. Not only have the Florida cougars (called Florida panthers) managed to maintain a small population in their refuge north of the Everglades, but cougars are now showing up in the eastern Appalachians, especially in Virginia. After the disappearance of deer due to overhunting in the mountains, deer were restocked in forested areas, and, since then, there has been a flurry of reports of cougars once again.

The question is whether these returning cats are re-establishing themselves or, perhaps, still in flight mode. From 1992 to 2014, records declare that 151,863 cougars in the lower forty-eight states have been killed, almost all by guns.

The latest estimates tell us that there are about thirty thousand cougars in the lower forty-eight states and about four thousand cougars in Canada. I say "about thirty thousand," but the estimates start at ten thousand and range up to fifty thousand. And I say "about four thousand" cougars in Canada, but estimates have gone as high as nine to ten thousand. Cougars are very hard to spot and therefore very hard to count.

They have made a comeback in British Columbia, where approximately thirty-five hundred live. Almost nine hundred of these cougars inhabit Vancouver Island, which makes this habitat the highest concentration of cougars in the world. Alberta currently has a viable population, but with such an extractive economy under way (oil, gas, mining), it's anyone's guess how long the cougars can hang on. They have also returned to Southwestern Saskatchewan and number about 350 for the province. This will be a surprise to some, but cougars have been spotted in Saskatchewan's accessible mid-north. Added to this are small, intact populations in Manitoba and the Yukon. I've seen reports on sightings in Central and Eastern Canada, but I have yet to see updates on cougar populations.

Sadly, because North Americans are expanding their towns and suburbs and living more and more on rural acreages, moving more and more into cougar territory, these miracle survivors are once again endangered. Some readers might think that my sentiments here are misplaced. Why, they might ask, should a few cougars stand in the way of progress?

Diane Josephy Peavey contends with the complexities of this question in her essay, "The Deer with the Long Tail." She lives on a sheep and cattle ranch in Western Idaho's mountainous High Five Canyon. Her story begins with the discovery of thirty-five slaughtered sheep on her land, killed by a marauding cougar. This slaughter comes after a ban on hunting cougars and the resultant increase in cougars in the area. Competing, as they do, with other cougars for mule deer and bighorn sheep (their prey of choice), the cougars had wiped out most of these animals in certain areas. Next, they depleted the elk herds, and finally, they had been forced to go far afield in search of food. Inevitably, the cougars turned to domestic animals. By the mid-to-late 1990s, there were dozens of instances of cougars slaughtering domestic sheep and other farm animals. While these attacks were going on, the towns and cities were expanding to such an extent that cougar habitat was vanishing. The lives of people who lived on the land were also compromised by this human invasion. "Follow the predator losses on the map," says Peavey, "and you will trace the regions of new growth." She felt that there were fewer places in her region to "breathe and roam free." She continues, "But those of us who live here gain our strength from wild lands. It is why we stay, even in the face of punishing economic odds. And although we are horrified at the sight of dead lambs in a mountain meadow, we are also appalled by the confusion of housing and industrial sites crowding the edges of our lives. So we hold out for open space, hoping that in the end it will save us, wildlife and humans alike."

My fascination with cougars was renewed, later in life, when I was the writer in residence at Haig-Brown Heritage House in Campbell River, on Vancouver Island. In Roderick Haig-Brown's well-stocked library, I found an old copy of an early novel he had written entitled *Panther* (1934). The research for this work of fiction came from his apprenticeship on Vancouver Island with a renowned mountain lion hunter named Cecil "Cougar" Smith, and from Haig-Brown's own short-lived career as a mountain lion hunter. What I admired most about the novel was his success at writing the story from the cougar's point of view. It felt like anthropomorphism with a difference, and I could not put it down.

One night, during our stay in the Haig-Brown house, Kever and I were about to climb into bed. We had just opened our bedroom window when we heard a caterwauling scream from close by—frantic, like that of a 1950s movie heroine being murdered—only much louder. I remember Kever's open-mouthed expression of alarm, and she remembers mine. The scream came from the direction of our back lawn, which lay parallel to the Campbell River.

I phoned a friend we had made out there, a man who had lived among alpha predators for many years. I asked him if that scream was what I thought it was.

"Well, Dave," he said, "it weren't no squirrel."

On my walk the following day, about a mile upriver from the Haig-Brown house, one of the hikers told me to watch out for a cougar. She reported that there had been several sightings nearby. For my own reasons, I did not tell her about the shriek in our back yard. It was the only time I heard that glass-shattering cry. Later, another wildlife enthusiast told me that it might have been a female yowling out her readiness for breeding.

When I'm in the bush, I'm frequently caught up in my fascination with animal tracks. This is especially true in cougar territory. I'm always on the lookout for signs of activity. A cougar's tracks are almost the size of a wolf's, but rounder and with a prominent heel pad behind the four digits. A large male cougar's print can measure four inches (nine centimeters) long by four inches across. Like most cats, cougars retract their claws so their prints reveal little or no evidence of their very large claws. The lynx is another cat that retracts its claws and leaves no sign of them in its prints. Though much smaller than a cougar, the lynx has proportionately huge paws but very small heel pads behind the four digits.

I'm telling you this in preparation for my next story, whose plot points are punctuated by paw prints. It happened on an April morning in 2018, when Kever and I were hiking with our Saskatoon friends Dawna Rose and Ian Dowl. We had chosen a West Coast trail that took us from a rain forest to a high rocky promontory.

As we plodded through the forest, I noticed a tiny stream running parallel to our path. Near the stream and beside the path were some muddy and sandy patches—great places to spot tracks of local fauna. That day I found a few deer prints, but nary a sign of a cougar.

Ian asked me what I was looking for.

There had been some rain the night before; therefore, many of the tracks I spotted in these open patches were recent. But, like I say, nary a cougar.

Dawna asked me what I was looking for.

Kever answered both of them. "He's looking for cougar tracks."

"Really?" said Dawna with mock skepticism. Further into the forest, I found a gorgeous muddy patch with no tracks of any kind. This unmarked muddy patch happened to be where the path forked. The right fork wound out of the forest and up into a rocky promontory with a remarkable view of the terrain below and the ocean beyond, a perfect place to stop. After a lively lunch we headed back down the same path. By force of habit I once again checked the same trackless, muddy patch.

"What are you looking for?" said Dawna.

"What are you looking for?" said Ian.

Kever got down on hands and knees and delivered the verdict.

"How could you have missed this one?"

"I didn't miss it," I said.

As we stood there staring at a perfect cougar track, we may have come to the same realization. Above us was the trail towards the ridge where we had eaten our lunch. The imprint of the animal's paw was pointed in that direction. So our recent visitor must have given us at least a sniff or a glance. Needless to say, this was the freshest cougar track I had ever seen.

During my hiking days on the West Coast, several times I received this morsel of wisdom from the people who lived nearby: *You never see them but they always see you.* This bit of wisdom had sounded like a cliché to me. *How do you know they're watching you if you don't see them?* On that hike we took with Dawna and Ian, I must have taken that rainforest axiom to heart.

On that same stretch of coastline, there are many sumptuous trails. On another occasion, Kever and I chose a shorter walk, a one-hour hike. We had to keep it short because of a dinner engagement with friends who lived a few miles away. Our trail snaked through an impressive jumble of coniferous and deciduous trees. There was no one around. To our right, the rainforest towered, and to the left was the ocean, lapping a rocky beach. I had to urinate, so I left the trail, stepped over a huge red log, and peed into some salal bushes.

We continued up the trail and were quite taken by the magic of this looming forest and the calm sea. At the half-hour point, we turned around as planned. Even though we were simply retracing our steps, heading back was just as enchanting. But ten or so minutes from the trailhead, I stopped abruptly. I was standing a few feet from the big red log where I had urinated on the first lap of the walk. I smelled something foul that I had never encountered before. Kever smelled it too. A great effluvium rose from the salal and the mossy rocks, and it curled like mustard gas into our nostrils.

"Good God!" cried Kever, perhaps tactfully, "what did you have for breakfast?"

Later, we told our dinner hosts, Jeanette Taylor and Gerry Coté, and their friend Annette Yourk, the intimate details of our walk. When I uttered the word *effluvium*, they broke out in a triumphant chorus of *Aha!* I knew in advance what they were going to say.

One by one, back and forth, they explained the phenomenon to us. A male cougar is territorial, and if another male whizzes on its territory, it will come back with the foulest olfactory rejoinder in its arsenal. For men who hike around Vancouver Island, there might be a lesson here.

٭

Just for the record, I should add that close to half of the sixty-seven recorded cougar attacks in the twentieth century in North America—fatal and non-fatal—have occurred on Vancouver Island. *You never see them but they always see you.*

٭

October, 15, 2013. A bright, beautiful day. We were driving through Saskatchewan parkland. Our friend, the artist Clint Hunker, had invited us and some other friends to a Thanksgiving dinner at his cottage in the Wakaw valley. This is about an hour's drive northeast of Saskatoon. In the car with Kever and me were our son Will and a hiking buddy of ours named Steve Whitehead. It was high noon when I turned off the highway and onto a freshly graveled road. I was bored with driving. A hundred metres ahead of us, an animal stood crouched in the gravel on the left side of the road. I announced its presence yawningly: *Critter up ahead, twelve o'clock.*

Lynx,
front track in muddy soil

Cougar,
front track in muddy soil

The animal's rump was facing us. Somebody's pet? It shifted its body towards the ditch, offering us a side view, and it seemed to have grown longer. Speculations poured from the back seat. A mink? A fisher? A raccoon? A skunk? No. A fox? A beaver? No. The animal crouched on the gravel and stared into the ditch. An otter? A wolf? I eased off the gas pedal and now the animal was looking our way. I noticed the long upward-curving tail and realized, with amazement, what we were gawking at. I was reluctant to say, because I thought I would sound like a flake. The animal slunk towards the bush.

Kever, bless her, named it for me. "It's a black cougar."

The four of us agreed. This animal was a black cougar.

The big cat seemed to flow into some heavy bush. We stopped the car near to the spot where the cat had been crouching. I was hoping to find a distinct paw print, but on the fresh gravel there was little to see except a few shapeless craters. Down in the ditch there was a network of raised ridges. Pathways, burrowed just below the surface of the soft ground, likely the work of pocket gophers. Perhaps, just before we disturbed it, the cougar had been sniffing out these rodents for a noonday snack.

Readers familiar with cougars may look upon our sighting that day with some skepticism. In the face of claims of black cougar sightings like this one, some cougar experts will claim these sightings are bogus, delusions, cases of mistaken identity, or outright lies. Other experts, hearing of these claims, will admit that melanistic varieties, though exceedingly rare, do exist.

Later on, I spoke with a tree faller on the West Coast who spotted a black cougar near his work site. He had lived in cougar country for almost five decades, and he struck me as an entirely credible witness. Three of my cabin neighbours further north at Little Bear Lake also claim to have seen a black cougar, fifty feet away on a narrow bush road. In both cases, these people saw the cats in clear daylight at a close distance from where they sat in their vehicles.

In the same week that I reported our black cougar sighting to a conservation officer in Saskatoon, another officer phoned me from the Wakaw Lake region to hear my story. He interrogated me in some detail, and then confessed that he'd never seen a black cougar. I asked him whether he'd ever heard reports of cougars in the Wakaw Lake area.

"Oh yes," he said. "I examined a cougar kill there, but I never saw the cat."

"When was that?" I said.

"Just this week."

I pay attention to all stories about cougars. Here's one from the *Saskatoon StarPhoenix* in 2016. It's about "Southwest Saskatchewan's cougar problem." I have noticed that in some circles, the word *problem* has been gradually phased out in favour of the more euphemistic term *issue. Government sources close to the President claim that he has issues with Black voters.* Issue is a soft word. It rhymes with tissue.

But for cougars, who don't vote or sue people, politicians still roll out the big one: "Southwest Saskatchewan has a cougar problem." In this article, Environment Minister (later Premier) Scott Moe announced "new predator control measures" that gave conservation officers "the power to hire local experts or 'trained houndsmen' to shoot, trap, or scare off problem animals." The reality behind this statement was that professional cougar hunters (a.k.a. houndsmen) do not waste their time trying to scare off cougars. In Saskatchewan and the rest of Western Canada, they kill hundreds of cougars by trapping and/or shooting them. Since Moe's 2016 announcement, I have attempted to get as close as possible to some of the sources of this disquieting situation, but so far my only evidence is hearsay from locals. In the United States, we know that about three thousand cougars are killed annually, mostly by hunters. In Canada, no such statistics are kept. During one of my months of interviews, a cougar hunter was said to have dispatched over a hundred cougars in a two-year stretch. According to another interviewee who helped researchers dart and collar eighteen cougars in Southwestern Saskatchewan, hunters and ranchers up in the Cypress Hills killed approximately fifty cougars in 2018.

If I were a rancher, married with small children, and living in or near the Cypress Hills, I would probably keep a rifle handy. Cougars, on occasion, can be dangerous to humans. But this is not to say that Saskatchewan has a cougar problem. We have problems maintaining elder care in this province. We have problems caring for the mentally ill. We have problems caring for the poorest of our people, especially up north, where even clean drinking water is denied them. We live in the presence of a glaring disparity between the rich and poor. As many Indigenous people will frequently remind us, we have problems with systemic racism. Compared to other parts of the country, Saskatchewan has a drinking problem. We lead the country in per capita charges laid for impaired driving. We have a problem with opiate addiction. We have a problem with teenage suicide.

Saskatchewan has a murder rate that is well above the national per capita average. I call these *problems* because they eventuate in a lot of deaths, injuries, and personal and family tragedies. But, try as I might, I can find no record of anyone in Saskatchewan being killed, or even attacked, by a cougar.

For a bit of perspective on this subject, I turn to Jim Williams' recent study, *Path of the Puma* (2018). Williams, a wildlife biologist who lives in a mountainous part of Montana, studies cougar ecology. There are many more cougars in Montana than in Saskatchewan, but some communities, like the one where Williams lives, are more tolerant of them. Montanans do hunt and kill cougars, but some of these hunters also advocate for the preservation of cougar habitat. Sometimes a young male cougar might set up shop too close to a rural community, and Williams is called upon to remove the animal by darting or shooting it. But Williams spends much more of his time raising awareness and lobbying on behalf of cougars and their territories.

Williams is a lifelong student of ecology, the science that teaches us about the relationships at play in the natural environment; in his words, the "web of life that includes everything from bacteria and photosynthetic green plants to insects, deer, elk, and wolves." Williams is particularly interested in the crucial role played by the large predators in the ecosystem. "Every one of the parts is needed if the ecosystem is to function naturally. Predators aren't villains. They are indispensable."

Cougars and other large predators need a lot of uninterrupted wild space to carry on their quest for survival. Of all the endangered big cats on our planet (cougars, tigers, lions, leopards, cheetahs, jaguars), cougars have been the most successful at re-establishing themselves on the wild fringes of our world. These places include wilderness parks like Jasper, Banff, and Waterton-Glacier International Peace Park in Alberta, the Bob Marshall Wilderness Complex in Montana, and some wilderness parks in Southern Argentina and Chile. These parks are core habitat for cougars, wolves, bears, and also for the guanacos, deer, elk, salmon, and other animals that sustain them.

As Williams writes, the parks are "mind-bogglingly beautiful. They're home to pumas and ranchers. They're pressed on all sides by loggers, miners, farmers, and realtors, by climate change, and earth movers, and everywhere by humans. But what they have most in common, perhaps, is that they have impassioned champions—wildlife advocates, hikers and hunters, anglers and philanthropists, and of course biologists, working the path of the puma from the Yukon to Tierra del Fuego."

I haven't mentioned Yellowstone in the above list of cougar-friendly national parks, because over the past decade or so, the wolves in the greater Yellowstone ecosystem have begun to kill off and drive out the cougars. The two apex predator species have always been more or less at each other's throats, but in the Yellowstone ecosystem, the wolves have taken over the elk territories traditionally favoured by the cougars. Not only have they managed to invade cougar dens to kill off their kittens but they are pushing adult cougars into a state of starvation.

I've spent a lot of time in Eastend and Maple Creek, Saskatchewan, two towns on different edges of the Cypress Hills. These sometimes lengthy visits have allowed me to meet many of the local ranchers and retired ranchers. I've loved my exchanges with them during countless visits, especially their stories, and especially the stories told by the old-timers. So I'm sure these hardworking ranchers in Southwestern Saskatchewan could be convinced to lay off shooting cougars if I could just drop in on them and plead my case. I'm sure the ranchers in our province would like nothing better than having a bleeding-heart, city-dwelling writer of liberal persuasion come into their homes and demonstrate how they should conduct their affairs, especially on the cougar front.

I'm always on the lookout for ads in *The Western Producer* that might read something like this: WANTED: animal-loving city slicker to enlighten ranchers on how to maintain friendly relationships with marauding cougars. Degree in English literature preferred.

*

There is nothing wrong with fearing cougars in the wild. A measure of fear can be a great motivator to observe safety precautions in the bush—especially on behalf of children. But when you look at the statistics relating to human deaths caused by animal–human encounters in North America, you will find that the vast majority are caused by insects, dogs, and horses. In the United States, bees, wasps, and hornet stings cause an average of fifty-three deaths annually. Dog attacks account for thirty-one deaths per year. Horses account for an average of twenty human deaths per year.

In North America, over the past hundred years, there have been twenty-seven fatal cougar attacks. Seven of these occurred in California, and thirteen more were scattered over the American Northwest and Southwest. The remaining seven, from 1949 to the present, occurred in Western Canada: six in British Columbia and one in Alberta. This averages out to one death every ten years. The last time a person was killed by a cougar in Canada was 2001, when Frances Frost was tragically taken down by a cougar while cross-country skiing in Banff National Park.

As is probably clear by now, I have become an advocate for cougars and their habitats. Their presence in the ecosystems as a keystone predator is vital to preserve a balance between grazers and carnivores. Like the wolves, cougars keep elk, deer, and other herbivores from overgrazing their habitats. They prevent overpopulation among their prey. And let's face it, the cougar is as beautiful a wild creature as any of us is likely to see.

However, my love for these animals comes with a warning, especially for hikers who (like I used to) take off into cougar country unaccompanied. Carry a sheathed knife or a canister of pepper spray, or both, on your belt (and not in your packsack). Pay attention. Look for tracks, look for kill sites, check the path behind you. Look for signs of scraping on the ground. This is how they hide their scat and their partially eaten prey. Listen for soft and stealthy sounds.

I knew a lake in the Jasper Rockies that used to be stuffed with brook trout. It made for a vigorous hike but it was well worth the effort. One sunny morning in early fall, I set out west from Edmonton to revisit this lake. At this time the trout would be staging in the gravel near shore in their pre-spawning mode. On my previous trip to this lake I had run into a black bear, and since then I had heard from friends that other black bears and lowland grizzlies had been spotted near the lake. I had been told many times that hiking alone in the bush could be a chancy proposition, so on this day in 1968, I brought a rifle along with me, which was then and is now illegal in the national park. I no longer own any rifles because I think that there are better ways to stay safe in the bush. But on this occasion all I wanted was to have a go at those lovely brook trout.

I was staying with Mac Stewart, a friend who had a cabin in the park but whose job prevented him from joining me on the trail the next morning. The fly-fishing from shore was great. I caught and released about a half-dozen brook trout and kept two nice ones to take back to my friend's cabin. I cleaned them and tossed the guts to a family of mink that were foraging among rock ledges on the shore. An angler more mindful than I on that day might have placed the guts in a plastic bag for transport, or buried them, but these mink were clearly hungry for them, so I broke one of the rules of prudent fishing.

As I walked away, I had my rifle strapped over my shoulder, my fly rod in one hand, and the two trout on a stick thrust through their gill covers and out their jaws in the other. In other words, my hands were full and I smelled of fish. I had a basketball referee's whistle around my neck. In those days, in case of danger from a bear, or in case of getting lost, some of us woodsy types carried loud whistles. A lesson from childhood.

The hike to my car was about three miles. The trail takes you down from the lake through the forest to a small parking space by the road. Over half the trees along this trail are deciduous, and in the fall, the cast-off leaves of aspens cover the ground. Shuffling and crunching through the leaves, you cannot walk quietly.

I had gone about a mile down the trail when, from a ridge above me, I heard an animal, probably a deer, moving through the trees. I could only glimpse it descending through the bare aspens and berry bushes. As I continued along, the descent of this deer became more audible, and I remember thinking that wild animals were supposed to be noiseless movers. But the crisp fallen leaves would not allow the deer to approach quietly, and I kept walking, wrapped in a dream of oven-baked brook trout.

I stopped walking and peered through the aspens and dogwood at the fawn-coloured creature that approached me. The *approaching* part gave me pause.

It might have been about twenty metres away. Something about this situation made me uneasy. I raised the whistle to my lips and gave a mighty blast. The deer crouched down behind some berry bushes.

Even a clueless city guy, if he's done any camping and hiking, knows a few things about deer. They don't tend to follow people in the bush. When they have been whistled or yelled at, they don't crouch down behind the shrubbery. If even slightly alarmed, they bound away through the trees. This deer had a very long tail with a black tuft, and although it was out of sight, its tail swayed slowly back and forth above the bushes like a cobra to the music of a flute.

Oh, Jesus, it wasn't a deer.

I had not intended to troll for cougars that day, but I'd found one. I backed down the trail, hoping that my whistle had done its work. But the cougar followed. Then it crouched down in the open for a bit of eye contact, an appallingly beautiful cat.

About then, I remembered I had a loaded rifle hanging from my shoulder. I lowered my fly rod to the ground, dropped the trout, and took the rifle into both hands. I did not raise the rifle to aim it or even lever a shell into the breech. I simply stared at the cat, and it stared right back at me. The air from the trout lake to this point on the trail must have been saturated with the aroma of trout guts, and here was the result of my carelessness.

I don't know how long I stood there gawking at the cougar. I remember it as a very long minute. And I will never prove this to anyone, but it seemed to me that something passed between me and the great cat—a message of some kind. Maybe the message's content was that I knew what it was, and that it had stalked me, and because of this thing I held with both hands in front of my chest, I was not afraid. In fact, I wanted to stretch out the moment of our encounter—just as, right now, as I write these words, I want to hang on to this moment of gazing back through the years into those feral golden eyes.

But then I realized that my friend was waiting for me. I retrieved the stick with the two trout, picked up the fly rod, shouldered my rifle and backed on down the path. I turned my back on the great cat and walked the rest of the way to my car.

Cougar

CHAPTER 15

The Three Bears

*O*ne evening in June a long time ago, my friend Peter Hyndman and I were casting flies from the shore of Johnson Lake, about ten kilometres east of the Banff townsite. As the dusk began to gather around us, we noticed a large black bear approaching. I remember gazing at the bear as it plodded between us. It might have come within twenty feet of me, close enough for me to pick up its musky smell. The bear took a drink from the lake, looked around, gave us a sniff or two, and returned to the woods behind us. We resumed casting our flies. The prospects of hooking a rainbow trout were infinitely more interesting than gawking at a big old bear.

That was 1960. What interests me about that brief visit was our absence of fear, or even vigilance. We had somehow learned not to fear black bears. They used to arrive in large family groups to meet the trains at the CNR station in Jasper. On warm summer days, around the town or out on the grounds of the Jasper Park Lodge, bears young and old would lounge in the shade like a gathering of hobos waiting for a handout. My memory of these charming loafers extends from the late 1940s to the early 1960s. Black bears were everywhere in the mountains then, and their presence was welcome but almost uneventful.

Along with many other people who frequent the mountains, I changed my mind about black bears (*Ursus americanus*) and gradually learned to respect them, sometimes even fear them. Between 1960 and 1970, bears, or our *perception* of bears, went through a transformation from innocuous moochers to nuisances to dangerous animals.

If I had been a regular reader of newspapers in my teenage years in Alberta, I would have learned that in Jasper Park, in 1958, Barbara Coates, a seven-year-old, had been mauled to death by a black bear. I would also have read that in 1959, near the foothills community of Cadomin, Alberta, Lyndon Hooper had been killed by a black bear. In all likelihood, I probably heard about these attacks on CHED, a relentlessly cheerful Edmonton radio station. And if so, I would have shrugged off the news. In those days, gravitas was hard for me to process, and news reports on radio seemed to slip through my system like shit through a goose. *Mea culpa.* I never want to be that young again.

These two maulings came eight years before the mauling deaths (by grizzlies) of Julie Helgeson and Michele Coons at Glacier National Park in Montana. But, spurred by the rise in the number of human–bear encounters, national parks on both sides of the border took action. One of the changes was to put an end to open-pit garbage dumps that had encouraged bears to become habituated to human activity. Many a habituated bear was killed in the 1960s, and, more than ever before, tourists were urged never to feed them or leave food untended around their campsites.

Most of us are more familiar with *Ursus americanas*—the black bear, than with its larger cousins, the grizzly bear (also known as brown, silvertip, Kodiak) and the polar bear. The black bears far outnumber the two larger species, and they range in forested areas all over the continent from Southern Mexico to Northern Canada and Alaska.

The black bear is an intelligent and resourceful animal that eats almost anything in its way. It is mostly a herbivore and insectivore, but if voles or marmots are available, they will not turn up their snouts at them. Black bears also feed on animal carcasses in the spring, winter's leavings, and if there are deer or other ungulates in the neighbourhood, they will hunt and kill fawns, and elk and moose calves during the late spring and early summer. Then it's on to saskatoon berries and a large menu of other berries, plants, and nuts. Throughout the late summer and fall, the sugar in the berries that a black bear consumes combines with carbohydrates to produce the fat that insulates the bear during its long winter sleep.

Some years ago I was camping on a canoe trip with my friend Calder somewhere north of La Ronge in Northern Saskatchewan. We set up our tents next to a lake in bear country, and when I finally fell asleep, I was awakened by a noise that I could not or would not define. Perhaps a stealthy paw? My hatchet was close by on the floor of my tent. I stayed awake for a while, listening for more noise but finally fell back to sleep. Once again, I was awakened by the noise. This time I heard it when I was fully awake, a sound made by an animal and very close to my tent. I could only assume that a black bear was investigating our campsite. I dozed uneasily until dawn arrived, and when I felt less guarded about the night's noises, I crawled out of my tent and scanned my immediate neighbourhood. The mystery was solved when I looked at the ground. All about my tent lay an accumulation of freshly severed spruce cones. Gifts, you might say, from a hard-working or perhaps territorial squirrel in the trees above me. A damn squirrel!

My problem had been with the bear within. And this psychic bear, if I can call it that, has a long history among the settlers of this continent.

A prominent expert on bears named Mike Pelton likes to think of them as "silent shadows that travel through the human imagination just as they move across the landscape." Pelton cites the ubiquity of bear clans, bear icons, totems, and dances as evidence of their presence in early cultures and in our minds. This bear consciousness seems to have something to do with their great size, their shaggy coats, and their resemblance to humans. A bear on the lookout will rise on two legs, and a skinned-out bear looks like a human body. Not surprisingly, many Indigenous hunters up north used to disapprove of killing bears because they thought of them as close ancestors.

In England, according to Thomas Babington Macaulay, bear-baiting was a favoured diversion of upper and lower classes. By bear-baiting, I mean setting dogs on a chained bear for the entertainment of an audience. This barbaric and popular practice, foisted on captive black bears and European brown bears, was discontinued after Oliver Cromwell and the Roundheads came to power in 1642—and not out of compassion for the bears. Cromwell's Puritans hated the practice because it gave pleasure to their unruly political enemies. According to Macaulay, the Puritans "generally contrived to enjoy the double pleasure of tormenting both spectators and bear" by slaughtering the bears meant for baiting.

Roughly two centuries later, the attitude towards bears in England did an about-face. A sentimental attitude developed that has persisted well into our own time and onto our own side of the Atlantic. Thanks to many popular representations of bears as adorable children (*Winnie the Pooh*, "The Teddy-Bears' Picnic," and many more), bear-baiting in England has evolved into bear feeding in the national parks of North America. In the late nineteenth and early twentieth centuries, woodsy novelists—from Ernest Thompson Seton, James Oliver Curwood, and Charles G.D. Roberts to the immortal William Faulkner—were drawn to bears as central characters in their narratives. Many of these bears and other animals were carefully observed, but too many cubs became cute and adorable, and too many adult bears became humanized in various ways. At least some of these novelists' bear depictions were eventually deemed sentimental and anthropomorphic. "Nature fakers," John Burroughs and Teddy Roosevelt both called them.

In one such portrait, found in Charles G.D. Roberts' *The Heart of the Ancient Wood*, a huge black bear sow, whose cub has just died, discovers a child lost in the woods and suckles her back to health as she would her own cub. The two form a lasting bond in which the bear becomes the protector of the family. All too often, as in the case of Roberts's novel, these woodsy, occasionally realistic novels had literary pretensions. They went cautiously beyond the fanciful and innocuous portraits of bears in children's stories, but most of these early twentieth century bears were not allowed to be entirely ursine. Compare them with the bears in William Faulkner's classic novella, *The Bear*, and Sid Marty's more recent account, *The Black Grizzly of Whiskey Creek*, and you'll see what I'm driving at.

☙

My own recent encounters with black bears have been in the boreal forests of Northern Saskatchewan, where Kever and I have our cabin. She loves solitary walks along the trails adjacent to Little Bear Lake. She always arms herself with pepper spray in preparation for the bear encounter that never happens.

Until it did. This was in late August, when bears are feeding voraciously to fatten up before hibernation. She was walking along the Chris's Pond trail when she spied an adult black bear ambling happily towards her. She put up quite a ruckus, waving hands and yelling, and the bear took off into the bush at a frantic pace. She recounted this incident to John Russell, a wildlife biologist and bear expert from near Waterton National Park. John was a member of the famed Russell clan of bear aficionados. He told Kever that her black bear was probably going about its daily routine, and yelling at it, sending it off in a panic, was not necessary. John said that he would simply have stepped off the path and waited until the bear had ambled away.

Another time, Kever was kayaking through the weedy shallows at the southern extreme of Little Bear Lake. She was checking out the water lilies and other vegetation in a marshy segment of the shore when a large black face attached to a large black body suddenly popped up. This black bear had been feasting on cattail roots. Kever backpaddled in a hurry, and the surprised black bear fled twice as fast in the opposite direction. This is how it usually goes.

My most exciting, recent black bear encounter in that vicinity was on a fishing trip with my nephew, Nick Carpenter, from Toronto. We had canoed and portaged our way into the heart of the Gem Lakes to do some fishing. It was a bright, hot day, and we were trolling on the shadowy side of Diamond Lake. As I was paddling, I glanced shoreward into the cool gloom of the forest and became aware of a blackness in the cavernous dark of the shade. This mass of deepest black had a light brown snout. I slowly made out the shape of a truly magnificent porker of a bear; in fact, the biggest black bear I have ever seen, a boar that would easily have tipped the scales at over four hundred pounds. It stood motionless except for the snout, which followed us almost imperceptibly as we trolled past. Young Nick was impressed. This may have been the first wild bear he had ever seen. We trolled our flies back and forth along the same shoreline, and each time, slowly, the bear's great head pivoted to observe this strange spectacle.

I couldn't help wondering after a while whether the bear was as fascinated with us as we were with him, and whether his interest was somehow related to hunger. I debated this in my head. Curiosity? Hunger? Curiosity? Hunger? In the end, I chose to err on the side of caution. Across this pond, on the sunny side of the water, a comfortable distance from the giant bear, there was a steep hill. Beyond it, a trail led out of the Gem Lakes to where my vehicle was parked.

"Nick," I said, "do you think we could tote this canoe up that hill?"

"How come?"

I shared my view with my nephew that we should haul ass. Nick was young, lean, and obviously in great shape, and therefore the perfect companion for grappling a canoe up a steep portage. Up we went, puffing all the way, and on the drive home I carried the image of that massive animal, squatting plump among the trees. The bear's manner seemed peaceful, self-possessed and perfectly at ease. Whenever I summon him up, I think of Buddha and how he might, at that moment long ago, have chastised me for my anxieties.

Well, a Buddha with real big teeth.

I expect that John Russell—and Buddha too—would have kept on fishing.

John Russell's brother, Charlie, wrote a delightful book about a very special black bear: *Spirit Bear* (1994). I'm referring to *Ursus americanus kermodei*, most frequently referred to as the spirit bear or Kermode bear, and sometimes simply the white bear. In fact, as Charlie pointed out, it's a black bear that was white due to a rare genetic variation. Charlie's book is a lushly photographed account of his encounter with these bears at Princess Royal Island on British Columbia's North Coast. This colour phase shows up rarely among black bears all over the country, but our chances of seeing one would be somewhat better if we could find our way north of Bella Bella to the Spirit Bear Conservancy and environs. These bears were (and probably still are) sacred among the Indigenous people of the Northwest Coast. In another sense, they are sacred among ecotourists and animal lovers in British Columbia.

Clearly these white bears are not sacred everywhere they show up. I was once talking with a hunter from Colorado, who came frequently to Northern Saskatchewan to shoot black bears. The subject of spirit bears came up, and he told me that he had only seen one of them.

"It was only a little one," he said, "but I knew I'd never see another one, so I shot it."

This is what we tree-hugging bear lovers are up against.

In my many years, I've seen a lot of spectacular wildlife: grizzlies, wolves, cougars, moose, caribou, and so on. Most of those encounters felt like major events at the time, but inevitably, I've lost quite a few. The ones that remain in my memory bank are no doubt the most dramatic. Here is one more example from the summer of 1963, when I worked for the federal hatchery in Jasper National Park.

I was helping my boss, Art Colbeck, release a bag of trout fries into a weedy stretch near the shore of Celestine Lake, a body of water well off the beaten track. The rainbows in Celestine grow big, but I've never seen an angler there, other than myself. Art Colbeck and I were in a two-man rubber dingy about twenty feet from shore. Something caught my eye, and I looked up in time to see a big moose drinking at the edge of the lake. It was probably less than twenty metres away.

I tapped my boss on the shoulder and whispered, "Look at the moose!" At that very moment, the moose thrust up its head. Thrust its entire body up on two legs and sniffed the air. Not a moose but a colossal grizzly rising like Grendel, like Goliath, like King Kong, like whatever. There is no simile that can do justice to a big boar grizzly. He turned around and launched himself into the forest, and, like a mythic monster, set the saplings whipping left and right.

Welcome to grizzly country. Welcome to *Ursus arctos horribilis*, known variously as the grizzly bear, the brown bear, the silvertip, and the Kodiak bear.

With their research, their books, and the films made by and about them, Andy Russell and his sons John and Charlie have helped to bring these mythmaking giants to our attention. So have many other writers, including Sid Marty, with his excellent portrait of the bear in *The Black Grizzly of Whiskey Creek*. Marty's story is an object lesson in bear–human interactions. Sid Marty reminds me that the grizzly is a different order of animal from the black bear, one that tourists in grizzly country disrespect or encroach upon at their peril.

The book is a nonfiction account, fleshed out with deft novelistic effects. It is frequently narrated from the bear's point of view. Marty calls the bear Sticky Mouth, and in the first close-up we get of him, he is trudging down from his winter lair in the mountains towards a highway in search of food. Sticky Mouth lays up for a while and noses the night breeze in the very place "where he had last lain in the circling protection of his mother's great limbs, some seven or eight years earlier." The great bear dreams his way back to the "Motherdark and the safety of the winter den."

Marty's narration unfolds in the third person, preserving a slight distance from the bear's inner life, his ruminations, as it were. Some of Marty's metaphors pertain to human perceptions, but at this point, as the narration shifts into italics, it sinks into the bear's mind, and the language goes by turns lyrical, mystical, and strangely feral: "What he remembers first is darkness and in it the warm breath of the Motherdark, and the rich smell and pleasant taste of the Motherdark, the taste of warm fat that flavours the milky proteins that course through the blood, to expand into muscle and bone."

In sleep, the great bear remembers how he and his sibling "*rolled together and slept in a ball*," listening to the "*muffled tympanum of the Motherdark*." The mother bear is "*vast and soft everywhere and seemed to be of no end or beginning*."

When Sticky Mouth goes for his last feed, Marty's narration starts on the outside and, as he did before, moves inside to present the bear's interior monologue. The men who pursue him are a "Twolegs pack." One of the men is a smoker, "the Burning Grass One...going around with its mouth on fire all day long, leaving a trail of smoke."

What impresses me here, even beyond the evocative prose, is the combination of intimate knowledge of the grizzly and the empathy of Marty's portrait of this animal that kills and maims people who encroach on his territory. This intimate portrayal is right up there with the best of nature writing in English, past and present. Another example is Helen Macdonald's stunning portrait of a goshawk in *H is for Hawk* (2014) and John Vaillant's riveting tale of the pursuit of an Amur tiger in *The Tiger: A True Story of Vengeance and Survival* (2011).

Remember that bravura impulse I ascribed to young men in Chapter 4, "Lo, the Serpent," the one that leads them to harass and pick up rattlesnakes in order to show off in front of their friends? A similarly stupid impulse drives a young shutterbug to follow a mother grizzly from the highway into the woods, snapping pictures as he goes. *Holy crap, she's got a couple a big cubs! Let's get a closeup.* The grizzlies just want to forage in peace, but Irrepressible Sidney Snapshot dares himself to get closer and closer. The mother grizzly does not want him to step between her and her cubs—even if her cubs are 250-pound three-year-olds. Irrepressible Sidney Snapshot is just one of eight billion bewildered human beings, intent on consuming every acre of land on the planet until the wilderness has been neutralized. On the other hand, this mama grizzly is a rare

specimen, astoundingly beautiful, and frequently endangered—
primarily by people like Irrepressible Sidney Snapshot.

And me.

My first encounter with grizzly bears was in the summer of 1962,
when national parks were still using outdoor garbage dumps for the
disposal of human food waste. The phrase *habituated bear* was not yet
in common parlance. In spite of being an ardent mountain hiker, I had
never seen a grizzly. I knew they were out there in the woods or up in
the alpine meadows, but the grizzlies were very good at avoiding us.

I was a twenty-year-old student employed for the summer at
the Jasper Park Lodge. While in Jasper, I was also a member of a
folk-singing group, and one evening in early September found me
hiking from the Lodge to Trefoil Lake, lugging my banjo to a paid gig.
I had to hurry, so I was looking for a shortcut through the woods. A
horse wrangler near the trailhead recommended a route to the lake.

"Keep to the left," was his primary piece of advice. "Whenever
you find a fork in the trail, always take the left one—except the
place where there's *three* forks. Then you go right a fair piece and
then left again."

I nodded to him as though I were gathering in every detail. It
seemed like the polite thing to do.

"If you run into a lot of junk on the trail," he said, "you've gone
too far, you're in the dump. Don't go near that dump. Not now, not
in the evening, *and by the Jesus, you know why.*"

Yes, I told him. I knew why.

As the light began to fade, I found a discarded license plate lying on the trail. Then a discarded muffler. Then a rusted-out car engine. Oops. The fork I had chosen must have been the wrong one. It led to a meadow at the upper edge of the dump. This meant that the danger lay below that edge, right? I entered a clover meadow embraced on three sides by pine trees, and much to my relief, saddle horses were munching on the clover.

My banjo seemed to have grown heavier in its case, but I continued past the first group of horses and spotted what appeared to be an exit from the dump. I also saw, however dimly, a second gathering of horses foraging not far from this exit. Anyone who knew anything about horses and bears knew that the two would not hang out together, browsing the same small meadow. Knowing that I was safe, I charged straight for the exit gate.

A very loud male voice began to yell. The man seemed for some reason to be cursing at me.

"What the hell are you doing?" the voice roared.

Through the fading light, I made out the figure of a wrangler on horseback.

"I'm just heading for the exit," I yelled back at him.

"What?" he cried, incredulous.

"Over there by those horses," I said, pointing at the five near the gate.

"What horses?" he said.

I looked again, squinting in the fading light. Oh, shit. They weren't horses. All five had paused from their grazing and were observing me with some alarm. The biggest grizzly of the bunch began to approach me in a pigeon-toed sort of trot. I trotted in the direction of the wrangler, who was parked on his horse beside a different exit I hadn't noticed

"Wanna climb up?" he said.

No, I told him, my banjo was too heavy. So he turned his horse and began a slow cantor away from the dump and through the woods. Lugging my banjo, I cantered after him, and soon I was safe.

Had this wrangler not intervened, I might have been mauled that night. And five bewildered grizzlies would have been shot by the warden service. I carried that image of the five grizzlies the rest of the way to my gig at Trefoil Lake, and later into the Jasper Blues Pub, where lodge employees liked to gather after work.

And I've brought that image of my first five grizzlies all the way to this desk where, sixty years later, I write these words, still in awe of those bears, and still groaning at my youthful stupidity.

One last reflection. When I arrived after my gig that night at the Pub, I was determined not to tell anyone of my foolish dalliance with death. A young fellow, who seemed to know some of my friends, joined us at our table and ordered a beer.

He said, "Did you guys hear about the idiot at the dump tonight?"

We all leaned forward. Idiot + dusk + garbage dump = disaster.

"Apparently," said this new arrival, "some tourist came to the dump tonight to serenade the grizzlies. Drunk as a skunk. He had a frickin' guitar. Ripley's, I swear. He had a frickin' guitar. Bunch a cowboys had to rescue him."

I mention this coda to my foolish adventure because it exemplifies the grizzly's capacity for inspiring exaggeration, legend and myth. Even more than black bears, grizzlies amble through our consciousness with mythic power.

I had another grizzly bear encounter in the summer of 1966 at Num-Ti-Jah Lodge, forty minutes north of Lake Louise on the Banff–Jasper Highway. I've told this one at many a campfire. I was the lodge gopher (night cleaner, bellman, garbage dumper, night clerk, toilet plunger guy, courier), and I was happy to do most of these jobs without anyone's help. One evening, my boss Jimmy Simpson said he would accompany me to the dump, because a bear was in the vicinity. Jimmy was a horse wrangler and owner of the lodge. If my memory serves me, he had been a hockey player of some renown. In his forties he was still very athletic and fast on his feet. He drove me in the lodge half-ton to a big excavation at the edge of an alpine meadow and parked the truck about fifty metres from the edge of the dump. Jimmy honked his horn long and hard, and when he exited the half-ton, he made sure to leave the keys in the ignition. I got the feeling that Jimmy had done this before. We each grabbed a cardboard box and made our way to the edge of the dump.

No bears anywhere. Like synchronized circus performers, we heaved our boxes over the edge, and one of them, Jimmy's box, landed at the bottom of the pit. My box whacked the snout of a grizzly, and it came up huffing on its hind legs. The distance from my boots to the bear's snout was about the length of a football. We both ran. Lucky for us, the bear ran the other way.

Either the bear was trying to escape the confines of the pit and into the bush, or it was trying to exit the pit in order to chew the hell out of us. Jimmy may have been a renowned athlete, but in our run back to the half-ton, I easily outdistanced him. I climbed into the cab, started the engine, and as I drove the truck over the gravel, we watched the grizzly climb the steep slope of the pit and gallop into the bush. With each leap forward, the grizzly's belly rolled side to side. I could plainly see that I would have fit entirely inside that belly.

Charlie Russell was born into a generation of men who shot these creatures on sight. His grandfather Bert Rigall was a master marksman and gunsmith. His father, the outfitter and writer Andy Russell, was none too trusting of grizzlies but, as Charlie and his siblings were growing up in the mountains, Andy must have come to terms with his distrust, because he taught Charlie how to photograph and film grizzlies without shooting them. But from the start, Andy was an outfitter, and sometimes he would lead hunters on bear-hunting expeditions. While still a young boy, Charlie accompanied his father as a wrangler on these trips. At some point, he told his father he wanted to stop going on the hunting trips because he liked bears a lot more than he liked tourists. Thus began Charlie's lifetime love affair with *Ursus arctos horribilis*.

In his earlier book, *Spirit Bear*, there is a photograph of Charlie hunkered on the ground in his waders, relaxing in the woods. Beside him, maybe eight or ten feet away, a wild white bear reclines in roughly the same position. What strikes me here is how much they must have trusted each other.

Much later, in a video made by Jeff Turner, *The Edge of Eden: Living with Grizzlies* (2006), there is an oddly similar photograph of Charlie sitting on the ground, relaxing next to a bigger bear. This time, the bear sits much closer to Charlie, a large young grizzly that makes Charlie seem somewhat smaller. The grizzly, like the spirit bear in the first photograph, seems to be imitating Charlie's slumped position on the ground. But more likely, their similar positions are unconsciously taken. And there they are, rumps on the ground, kicking back in silent companionship, like old friends on deck chairs trying to decide where to go for a beer. This second photo was taken on the Kamchatka Peninsula on the northeast coast of Russia. Up there, as in Alaska and the Yukon, these animals are called brown bears, and although they are varieties of the same species of bear, the brown bears are much larger than our southern grizzlies. Nevertheless, in the photograph of Charlie and the brown bear, Russell seems even more comfortable with his latest bear. The photograph speaks eloquently of trust between two different creatures.

The book, *Grizzly Heart* (2002), written by Charlie Russell and Maureen Enns, with editing help from the novelist Fred Stenson, recounts the Russian odyssey of Charlie and his partner, Maureen, the photographer and painter. They spent six summers in Kamchatka, the most densely populated grizzly habitat in the world. The book documents their lives among the brown bears. Perhaps the central narrative of this book is the story of three bear cubs—Chico, Biscuit, and Rosie—sisters whose mother had been shot by a hunter. When Charlie and Maureen came upon them, they were cubs, caged and woefully neglected, likely to spend the rest of their foreshortened lives in a so-called zoo. Charlie and Maureen acquired the three cubs and took them by air to their cabin in Kamchatka. Their intention was to raise them from cubs to young adult bears.

One of Charlie's biggest challenges was to teach the cubs how to survive in the wilds. This meant teaching them how to locate their most nourishing food—pine nuts, sedges, and berries—and to catch spawning salmon and char. The cubs' mother had been killed long before she could teach them how brown bears fattened up for winter hibernation. The three cubs are at first mildly interested; they play at catching the fish and just gawk at them. On this first day of Charlie's fish-catching lesson, the cubs have already had a good feed (from Maureen and Charlie) before pursuing the fish. They simply let them go. So Charlie makes an enclosed trench out of a small creek, catches some char, and releases them into it. This time the three sisters go after the fish more seriously. Slowly, each of them learns to play this vital game. It's a lesson in independence.

Once the bears have tasted fish, they become ever more curious about how to catch them on their own. Charlie is their protector, their mother, and their mentor. The more the cubs learn what to feed on and how to find their food, the more he backs off so the cubs will gain their independence at an early age.

Under Maureen and Charlie's nurturing, the bears grow fast and gain courage. They begin to explore farther and farther away from the cabin and soon face the perils that other young bears confront in the north, including the very real threat of being killed and eaten by older rogue bears.

Charlie bonds deeply with Chico, the dark brown cub, who learns about hunting food faster than her sister cubs. Maureen bonds with Rosie, a light blonde cub who is always last in line on their many treks across the tundra. Rosie tends to explore new things while the others are moving along. She frequently gets lost. Maureen thinks of Rosie as the artist of the family. By the end of the first summer, all three of the cubs have become Charlie and Maureen's beloved children. As the snow begins to fall, the cubs drift off into the fog and the blizzards, dig a cave, and successfully hibernate. For several summers thereafter, the cubs return to visit with Maureen and Charlie, and the five of them maintain their early bonds. Much of *Grizzly Heart* is a love story between bears and humans.

Charlie and Maureen run into some serious opposition to their bear project from the Russian authorities. Some of these opponents are scientists and bureaucrats. Others are poachers. The two Canadians argue persistently that if you show respect for the bears, if you are calm in their presence and patient with them, they will start to trust you. In return, you will come to trust them.

Some of their Russian friends agree with Charlie and Maureen, both of whom, initially, had to come to terms with their own fear of bears. But their many opponents cling to the old beliefs, that grizzlies are ferocious and unpredictable towards people. The grizzlies are there to be shot for their meat, their gall bladders, and their hides. They were there to be hunted by men for the thrill, the manly conquest of killing a dangerous animal.

Charlie and Maureen functioned as advocates for their vision of tolerance and trust of brown bears, challenging the image of these animals as ferocious marauders. They strive to replace that fear-based idea of bears with an entirely different narrative. While in Russia, they struggle tirelessly against bear poaching. With their Russian friends, and with some of their detractors, they walk a lot of miles in bear country without fear.

And just in case there might be a rare lapse in ursine civility, Charlie and Maureen always carried canisters of pepper spray. Charlie built electric fences around their cabin and around his ultralight airplane to reduce the chances of coming into contact with the hundreds of Kamchatka wild bears. He also built the fences in small settlements for other people to keep the bears out and to reduce nasty human–bear encounters.

By the end of *Grizzly Heart*, we get the picture of a divided Russia on whether to slaughter brown bears for food and profit or learn to know and respect them.

That vociferous debate sounds a lot like the one that persists in North America between those who argue on behalf of hunting grizzlies as trophies and those who want humans to coexist peacefully with bears, however cautiously, in protected wilderness areas.

🐾

Polar bears, *Ursus maritimus*, are even bigger than the brown bears. They are not only the biggest bears in the world, they are also the largest carnivorous quadrupeds on the planet. The upper range of a brown bear's weight is 1,160 pounds (525 kilograms). The upper range for male polar bears is 1,760 pounds (800 kilograms).

Polar bears are also the least populous of North American bears, currently ranging from twenty-two to thirty-one thousand animals—which makes them by far the most vulnerable species. The global grizzly bear population is thought to be around two hundred thousand animals. The Polar Bear Specialist Group of the International Union for the Conservation of Nature (IUCN) did a study (2019) of polar bear populations throughout the world, including Russia, Denmark (Greenland), the United States (Alaska), Norway, and Canada. Sixty to eighty per cent of the planet's polar bears are to be found in Canada. The Specialist Group has divided the overall population of *Ursus maritimus* into nineteen groups of polar bears. Some of these groups are fading, some of them are returning to earlier numbers, some are lacking proper tabulation, and some of them are thriving. The IUCN's overall projection for the future of the polar bear, however, is discouraging: by the year 2050, their global numbers are expected to decline by thirty per cent.

The main reason for their projected decline is global warming. Polar bears are losing their ice, and the ice is their primary hunting ground. From around October (freeze-up time) to spring (the time of the big melt) polar bears prowl the northern ice, hunting mostly for ringed seals. In some habitats, they also prey on bearded seals, harp seals, and hooded seals. When the ice retreats in the warmer months, polar bears enter a long period of fasting, occasionally relieved by scavenging the blubber and meat of dead walruses and whales, as well by hunting caribou and smaller game. During times of food scarcity, polar bears also eat berries, grasses, seaweed, and waterfowl.

Regardless of how resourceful these great bears are at finding food during the warmest months, their warm season is growing longer, the ice is disappearing more rapidly, and the bears are becoming desperately hungry. In response, they must travel further south into the tundra, including into settlements and fishing camps, to find nourishment. This is the time when most polar bears are shot and killed. Puzzling as it may seem, there are still legal hunting seasons for polar bears in Nunavut and the Northwest Territories, as of 2020. Wikipedia reports that, over the past century, there have been only seven fatal polar bear attacks in North America—six in the Canadian North and one in Alaska.

Tourists are still travelling to Churchill, Manitoba, to see the polar bears. What they often behold is the skin-and-bones survivors trying to deal with a lack of ice for hunting and for food. An appropriate gesture for tourists in Churchill would be to bid these beloved bears goodbye.

In a remote region in Northern Saskatchewan, northeast of Buffalo Narrows, a forty-four-year-old woman camping with her family was killed by a black bear this summer (2020). Stephanie Blais was the mother of two young children. She is the first person to die of a bear attack in this province since 1983. Strangely, this tragedy hit the news while I was writing this essay. Even more recently, as I was concluding this account about bears (August 28, 2020), a visitor camping on Svalbard, the Norwegian archipelago about five hundred miles north of Norway's mainland, was killed by a polar bear. Both of these stories made international news—not because there is a plague of bear-inflicted deaths around the world, but for other, less obvious reasons. Deaths attributed to wild predators are more unusual, more horrific, more spectacular than death by heart attack, cancer, or even motor accidents. Good news is no news. Bad news travels fast. Horrific stories travel faster still. Such fatal bear attacks, however infrequent, generate a disproportionate amount of fear and vigilance, which translates into a disproportionate slaughter of these animals.

In my early research, I read two books about bear predation. They share a similar title: Stephen Herrero's *Bear Attacks* (2003) and Erin McCloskey's *Bear Attacks in Canada* (2008). Herrero's book is rich in information about the evolution, the habits, diets, and dangers of black bears and grizzlies. McCloskey's book includes a riveting, well-researched section on polar bears, but is otherwise less encyclopedic in scope than Herrero's study. McCloskey opts for a selective approach on bear attacks and how to prevent them. At times, at least for me, reading these books made for a disheartening experience because, occasionally, they read like the crime report section of a large urban newspaper. Both books are very hard to put down. Edifying though they are on how to avoid bear attacks, I would rather read them after a wilderness camping trip than before. They both feature cover photos of enraged grizzlies, and it just gets more lurid as the pages turn.

But then we look at the statistics. Herrero reports that from 1960 to 1980, in North America, there were twenty-three deaths inflicted on humans by black bears. He also reports that from 1900 to 1980, again in North America, there were forty-one deaths attributed to grizzly bear attacks. He mentions that the North American black bear population is roughly ten times the number of grizzlies, the latter species being endangered in most of its habitats. So the black bear's record of human slaughter is proportionately much smaller than that of the more short-fused grizzly bear. Herrero analyzes these numbers in terms of hikers in grizzly territory during the 1970s. For example, for every 1.3 million visitors to Glacier Park, Montana, one person was injured by a grizzly bear. In Yellowstone, during the same time span, there was one injury inflicted for every 1.5 million visitors. Herrero's book inspires nightmares; his statistics are another thing entirely.

In the past decade in North America, grizzly bears and black bears killed twenty-eight humans, ten of them in Canada. Again, in the past decade, the North American average has been 2.8 human victims per year, the Canadian average amounting to about one fatality per year. On the other side of the statistical story, in British Columbia between 1975 and 2016, humans (mostly trophy hunters, resident and foreign) have killed 13,804 grizzlies, an average of 329 grizzlies per year.

If these statistics read like the mopping-up exercise after a one-sided war, it's not far from the truth. We human beings are not just the victors in an all-out war against the beasts that frighten us; we are the ultimate cold-blooded predator on the planet. Which brings me to the most disquieting statistic of all. In recent times in the United States, the annual murder toll is roughly sixteen thousand people. In Canada, over the same period, between six and seven hundred people are murdered annually. This is a proportionately smaller figure but nothing to be proud of. In North America, in an average year, fatal human predation on other humans (in urban or rural areas) occurs approximately six thousand times more frequently than fatal wild bear attacks on humans. To put it another way, while humans are a huge and pervasive threat to the survival of some of our most magnificent and storied creatures, large wild predators are becoming so rare that you can count yourself lucky to see one apex predator in the wild in your entire lifetime. To put it yet another way, your chances of living to a ripe old age may well improve if you keep chugging along wilderness hiking trails, or snowshoeing through the northern boreal forest, or sleeping in your tent in big-furry-beast country.

All of which brings me to the story of Goldilocks and the Three Bears. There are many versions of this tale, but I grew up with this one. A bear family consisting of Momma, Poppa and Baby Bear take a walk from their home to let their breakfast porridge cool. In comes Goldilocks and helps herself to their porridge, then she tries out the family's chairs. She breaks the smallest chair and then gives the bears' beds a try. She falls asleep just before the Bear family returns from their walk. They are bewildered by the home invasion, the pilfered porridge, and the broken chair, and then they discover

Goldilocks in their cub's bed. Eeek. Goldilocks jumps up and skips out of the house, free to help herself to someone else's porridge.

I never liked Goldilocks. She's too Goldi-centric. Perhaps her parents told her that she was a very special little girl and, with her many charms and winsome ways, she was entitled to the very best wherever she went. And the little sap *believed* them! Goldilocks is the only human being in the story, and she reminds us all too well of who runs the show in our present day anthropocene. The bears' habitat is *her* playground. The Goldilocks story sums up what human beings have done to the terrestrial wilderness, the ocean, the atmosphere, and now the climate. On gloomy days I can't resist the conclusion that Goldilocks is us.

Grizzly

CHAPTER 16

Epiphany

*I*n John Keats's poem, "Ode on a Grecian Urn," the poet envisions a sculpted urn with images of young lovers in pursuit and flight, panting for embrace—and, of course, the things that happen after the embrace. But these ardent lovers will never embrace because they are frozen in marble. They will, for all eternity, be almost embracing. If there is such a thing as unconsummated bliss, these kids have it in spades.

You might wonder why I'm telling you this.

Many winters ago, probably around the end of the millennium, my friend Calder and I drove to the boreal forest, four hours northeast of Saskatoon. Late in the afternoon we arrived at the tiny settlement of Little Bear Lake. If it wasn't completely snowbound, it was the next closest thing. This was March, but that far north, it was still midwinter. Calder managed to park his car somewhere near his driveway, and we waded through deep snow to his front door. He unlocked the door, and with squeaking boots we shuffled into the cold cabin. We unloaded our stuff and I did some hasty shoveling, and Calder lit the fire in the stove, filled the kettle with water brought from the city, and put on supper.

As the night came on and the cabin warmed enough so that we could unzip our parkas, Calder and I got into the scotch. Eventually we arrived at the stage where, although we could still pronounce many of our syllables, we had given up on clarity. During a lull in the conversation, which may have occurred when Calder went to the can, I became aware of a strange jubilance vying for my attention.

Slowly, falteringly, this thing turned into a thought which, if not exactly lucid, demanded (*hicket!*) further attention.

1) Calder and I were sitting in his cabin in late winter. 2) The forest was laden with several feet of snow. 3) The cabin, in turn, was surrounded by trout. *Wha?* 4) Okay, the cabin was surrounded by frozen trout ponds: Road Lake (rainbow trout) to the north; Cora Lake (rainbow trout) to the east; Dorothy Lake (rainbows, brook trout) to the northwest; Kit Lake (rainbows), a good hike to the west; the Gem Lakes (brook trout, brown trout, rainbows), another good hike to the west; Sealey Lake (brook trout and rainbows), a short drive south of us; and Shannon Lake (brown trout) twenty-five minutes' drive to the south.

Which brings us to 5) In addition to these and other trout ponds, like the veins and arteries connected to my heart, there were several streams winding through various valleys in the frozen proximity of Calder's cabin, none farther than sixty kilometres away and every one of them filled with brook trout. 6) Not to labour the obvious, but Calder and I were absolutely surrounded by trout waters, all of them frozen over and therefore inaccessible to fly-fishing. 7) Nevertheless, the trout were moving slowly beneath the ice by the tens of thousands, moving their tails and working their gill covers, all of them from three to seventy kilometres as the raven flies, tailing in the currents, drifting through the littoral zones, dreaming, as I was, of spring. 9) I was surrounded by uncountable silvery godlings. 10) No, I was pie-eyed and plastered, and therefore surrounded by silvery godlings.

"Whadya mean?" said Calder, who was evidently back from the can. I must have been muttering my thoughts aloud.

"Calder," said I. "Calder, I have had an epiphany."

"Good for you," he said, sitting himself with some difficulty at the table.

"Seriously. I have had an epiphany."

Calder stared at me with bewilderment, skepticism, and concern. All three.

"At this particular juncture," I said, waving my hand to gesture all around us, "at this particular juncture, we are surrounded by trout."

"You mean over by the sink?"

"Nonono, in the lakes and streams all around this cabin. Surrounded by trout. Uncatchable...beneath the frozen...beneath the frozen depths of winter...like the..."

"Like the what, Carpenter?"

"Like the panting lovers...lovers in pursuit...on the Grecian urn."

As I sat there, still dreaming of spring, Calder scratched his head and looked down at the floor, as though he were charting a path away from this conversation.

Lately, I've been wondering about my fascination with predatory animals and wildlife in general. When did this start? What keeps bringing me, a city boy, back to the bush? Back to the blue highways, hiking trails, back to Bob's cabin, and then to my own cabin up north, and back to the possibility of encountering wild animals. Genetically speaking, it may have started with my two Saskatchewan grandfathers, Artie Parkin and Henry Stanley Carpenter. They both came out from Ontario in 1905. My two grandmothers, Ethel Parkin and Jessie Carpenter also came out (under protest) from Ontario. In the early decades of the twentieth century, roughly from 1905 to 1940, Artie was a renowned hunter and fisherman, at least around Saskatoon and points north of there. If he is remembered at all, it is because in the 1920s and 30s, he presided over the Straight Shooters, a club for boys to learn about gun safety, marksmanship, and the joys of hunting and fishing. In Regina, from 1905 to about 1930, my other grandfather, H.S. Carpenter, was a dominion land surveyor who spent many a spring, summer, and fall camped with survey crews from rural Southern Saskatchewan to Northern British Columbia. More by necessity than obsession, he was outdoorsy, and he taught my father and my uncles how to fish for pike and pickerel, and how to hunt for grouse and mallards.

In their separate families, my mother and father grew up with stories about tent-raiding bears and ill-tempered moose in Northern Saskatchewan. My parents courted in and around Pike Lake, near Saskatoon, and at Waskesiu Lake, north of Prince Albert. They took my brother and me tenting when we were toddlers. My father took us fishing for pike, and my mother (not always cheerfully) cleaned our catches. Our father taught us how to pluck ducks and upland birds, and until I was about eight years old, I thought this chore was meant as a privilege.

A year or two later, on summer holidays at Lake Wabamun (west of Edmonton), my older brother and I spent many an hour in an ancient, leaky rowboat, vying with each other over who could catch the most pike. That summer, possibly 1953, he caught thirty and I caught a mere thirteen. At that time, I found myself looking around for some way of fishing that my brother might not pursue. I was tired of casting in his shadow. My parents had given me a subscription to *Outdoor Life*, and I read the fly-fishing stories by luminaries such as Joe Brooks and Tom McNally. These fly-fishing scribes kick-started what I think of now as my literary education. As well, around that time, I watched a documentary about Roderick Haig-Brown catching a big steelhead on a fly rod. What most caught my attention were the loops fore and aft that he made with his flyline. He hefted it back behind him, paused for a second to let the line straighten out, and then whipped the line forward in a flat unraveling loop across the flow of the river. It was almost unbearably beautiful. I knew from that moment forward what I was here for, or so it seemed to me then.

In school I was bored to distraction. *David is off somewhere*, my older brother would say. Yes, in the classroom, I was frequently off somewhere, but as a student of fly-fishing, I went to the head of the class.

It started with my father, who bought me my first fly rod and drove me and my friend Hyndman to places like Jasper, Rocky Mountain House, and Ricinus. Yes, Ricinus: a clutter of tiny cabins on the Clearwater River, east of the Central Alberta Foothills. In the spring of 1955, wading in Mud Creek, a half-hour drive from Ricinus, I caught my first trout on a fly, a dry fly known as a black gnat. I managed this by sneaking up on an old fly fisher from Red Deer named Mr. Brown. I watched him catch a brook trout on a short cast. He netted it, whacked it, and slipped it into his creel, as though this stuff was easy as pie. I spotted several of his fat brookies in there, including a fifteen or sixteen incher. His advice to me was as follows: *Keep as low as you can so the trout don't spook. Cast upstream above the rises.*

The rises?

The splashes from the feeding trout.

When he trudged upstream, I waited for the trout to resume rising. Then I cast my black gnat a few feet upstream from a rise and caught a foot-long brook trout. I was thirteen. This may sound like a pretty pedestrian rite of passage, but for a young man in the throes of a full-blown trout fetish, it was anything but pedestrian. It was more like a bar mitzvah.

The point is that I come to this meditation on wild predators from my own predations with a fly rod. I took fly tying and fly casting lessons in an old school gym because of the trout. At age seventeen, when I was a freshman at the University of Alberta, I applied for summer jobs in the mountains because of the trout. A few years later, I worked as a grunt in the Jasper fish hatchery, slicing and grinding up cow livers, because of the trout. I hiked into the mountains with friends, and we camped and shivered through stormy weather in grizzly country, because of the trout. I continued to cultivate my friendship with Peter Hyndman, who was my political opposite and much smarter than me but who also had an obsessive love of fly-fishing, because of the trout.

The flies I tied had to bear some resemblance to the insects that trout fed on: caddisflies, jassids, grasshoppers, bees, mayflies, stoneflies, nymphs, leeches, minnows, and scuds. So fly-fishing had an entomological as well as an ichthyological dimension to it. Up in the Rockies, the trout seemed to inhabit the clearest of lakes and spawn in the most limpid of streams. (The preferred, if not obligatory, modifier in fly-fishing magazines for these streams was *gin clear.*) The trout lived where the water was healthiest, richest in oxygen, full of nutrients like calcium and potassium, abundant in bug life. The presence of trout heralded the most pristine and robust of ecosystems. Because fishing for trout often took me into the wildest places and the most scenic landscapes that I had ever beheld, fly-fishing had an aesthetic dimension to it as well as an ecological one.

And so it went, my trout-driven education included acquiring many skills: pitching tents, building campfires, using a compass, and paddling a canoe. At the tender age of seventeen, I could also cook a trout over a fire on a green stick. All of these exhilarating lessons were impelled by visions of rainbows, cutthroats, brown trout, and brookies. Their presence in the streams bespoke something perfect at the heart of all creation.

Wading after trout took me from my matter-of-fact existence as a bewildered and bored young student to being an enchanted young man in the gallery of nature. Alford Creek, Patricia Lake, the Raven River, Johnson Lake, Louise Creek, the Upper Bow River—these were my Louvre, my Frick, my Taj Mahal. The creeks especially were live and flowing theatres of predation and flight where, to nymphs, flies, and minnows, hungry trout were the top predators. My own predations on the trout depended on my skill at creating an illusion: an imitation of a mayfly landing on the surface that would trick a

feeding trout below. Usually the trout were not fooled, but sometimes the magic wand was working, and when it worked, I felt as
though, in some exhilarating way, I had arrived.

I was wrong. I had not arrived; I had only just boarded the train.
Somewhere along the way, the wildlife and the habitat had begun to
claim my attention in a way that rivaled my love for fly-fishing. This
gradual shift from a simple trout fixation towards a wider engagement with wilderness and wildlife was so gradual that it seemed to
have no starting point. Was it my first encounter with a grizzly? My
first sighting of a prairie rattler? Or that evening outside of Jasper
when I gazed at the family of cougars? Who knows? But when my
father began taking Hyndman and me fishing for trout in prairie
pothole lakes and foothill streams, a different kind of door began to
open to bigger rooms than I could ever have imagined. But my study
of predacious creatures also began because of the trout.

Does this make me special in some way? No, but it has made the
animals very special.

Every June and every September I gather with Bob Calder and
Len Findlay to go fly-fishing. As we grow older, the trout haul gets
smaller, unless Warren Cariou comes along, and then the trout haul
approaches respectability. Warren is younger than us by about three
decades. He was an exceedingly bright student of mine during my
teaching days at the University of Saskatchewan, and now he is a
professor at the University of Manitoba. Partly because of his work
with Indigenous writers, elders and storytellers, he is very much in

demand. He is also a superb trout fisherman, and everyone with a fly rod, it seems, also wants to fish with him.

As Calder, Findlay and I lurch through the last of our seventies, we have become aware of the limits to our energies. Calder's laughter is youthful, and his appetite for world news voracious, his frequent political reflections as perceptive and scathing as ever. He's still writing, but he walks with great difficulty. In old age, Calder is all of us. Even in retirement, Findlay is still in many ways a piss-and-vinegar radical, younger in mind than in body, but always the last one to come off the lake as the cold and dusk move in, because he is too keen and too Scottish to do otherwise. Some days I am preoccupied with a litany of complaints about my health, not all of them merely neurotic. My leg cramps have become so painful that I can no longer manage a bellyboat. I have to use a tiny rowboat with a small electric motor, and I have to rely on my friends to help me get it in and out of the water.

The older we get, the better the fishing used to be, and the bigger the trout we used to catch. All four of us live in youthful expectation during trout season. Casting our lines in the trout water, even on unproductive days, we are still somehow about to get a strike. We are about to connect with the biggest *Salmo trutta* we have ever seen, a kype-jawed denizen the colour of dark gold, with tinges of olive green around the yellow fins, sprinkled all over with black spots and occasional red blotches, torpedoing slowly into the shallows, drawing our facial features forever in expectation. We are about to connect with the wild force of the universe that made us. *Shhh, don't scare it away.*

At this point, I'll resist any comparison between the uncatchable trout and the panting lovers in full frolic and flight on a Grecian urn;

that conceit might work a little better with scotch. But hold on for
the ride of your life, because sure as you're born, an encounter with
perfection is heading your way, the kind of engagement that tests
your resolve and keeps the old blood pumping.

CHAPTER 17

The Cabin that Saskatchewan Built

*E*ver since boyhood, I have loved cabins: the austere pleasures of northern solitude, wood fires crackling in the morning chill, the arias of calling loons, the mysterious world of the surrounding forest. The bear sightings, the soaring calls of howling wolves, the bellows of rutting moose, and so much more. This enthusiasm got revived one evening in June 1997, when my wife and I were on a working retreat. All day long, in a rented cabin, Kever had been labouring over a large painting and I over a manuscript. We took a walk down by the narrows of Little Bear Lake, four hours' drive northeast of Saskatoon, or twelve hours north of the Montana border.

"If we had a cabin," Kever said, "we could come up here just any old time." If we had a cabin. We could swim in a lake. We could heat it with the wood we chopped. We could go fishing all the time. *If we had a cabin.* The phrase had been popping up from both of us throughout the week. "We could work up here till midafternoon and then just go hiking," Kever added.

That day we had spotted a mother black bear and her cub crossing the highway. Two days before, on the last hour of our drive from town, we had spotted a large male bear feeding on clover beside the road. There were rumours of wolves north of Little Bear Lake. I was aching to see a wolf.

Something in the depths of my being tailed to the surface and snapped up Kever's suggestion. If this had been a movie, a wolf would be howling somewhere off in the hills. Taj Mahal would be singing *Ah'm a goin' fishin.*

Back then, the Little Bear cabins went for about $75,000, a heck of a lot of money. The lakeside ones went for $100,000, and the big ones with the boathouses probably went for twice that. We could afford none of these. But there was one woeful lakeside cabin that looked to me as though it might sell for a lot less. Its roof was sway-backed and it stood in a clearing like a tired old horse. On a chilly evening, we wandered past the place and halted by a garage on the next lot over that housed a workshop. Inside, the Baxter brothers, Dave and George, were enjoying happy hour and were resting after their labours. They had spent the day working on George's new cottage. A fire was going in the big wood stove. The brothers were the very picture of contentment.

What happens when an ordinary scene becomes endowed with magic? Here were two men, old enough to consider retirement, but still energetic, enjoying their drinks by the fire. We asked about the shack next door and were told that it belonged to a widow named

Dulcie Hill. I couldn't help but notice how relaxed these brothers were, how much they loved to build things, how friendly was their laughter, how the brothers warmed to the prospect of new neighbours. In the excitement of our quest for Mrs. Hill's cabin, I often thought of the Baxter brothers, walking ads for a vigorous retirement. Up at Little Bear, there were many handy guys of a similar age, happily engrossed in the building of cabins, garages, and storage sheds—an entire species of industrious retired guys. And one shack on a lakeside lot for the astounding price of $40,000.

Dulcie Hill was a plucky widow with firm ideas about cottage life. When the cottage owners of Little Bear met to review their waste disposal procedures, they agreed to do away with all primitive toilet structures. By law, everyone had to have a septic tank. The effluent would be hauled away in a honey wagon to a sewage lagoon off in the woods. Composting toilets were yet to become available up north, so it was septic tanks or nothing. The government health and sanitation official who had come to the meeting of cottage owners would have it no other way. Dulcie Hill was the only holdout in the room. When she stood to speak, forty pairs of eyes turned uneasily her way.

"I got me a little house behind the house that works just fine, thank you very much," said Dulcie. "Besides, if a moose can shit in the woods, so can I." She sat down to a silent room.

But, in 1997, Dulcie was finally ready to sell. Her cabin was on a long, narrow lot that ran northwest down to the shores of Little Bear Lake. Every evening, Kever and I would walk by and see the cabin bathed in sunset radiance, an incandescence from blue–green and deep orange to dark violet. The flaming washes of primary colour were as brazen as the bellies of spawning brook trout. In the evening,

Dulcie's cabin paraded these colours before our awestruck gaze. How could anything so perfect be so cheap? There was an answer to this question but it was some time coming.

Little Bear Lake lies north of the Torch River, just below Canadian Shield country on the sandy terrain of the accessible mid-north. Eskers wind through the forests like the backs of great serpents. These sinuous ridges left by retreating glaciers embrace the many lakes and ponds at Narrow Hills Provincial Park. The water is packed with nutrients and is as pure as any mountain lake you could ever hope to see. Correction: that you could ever hope to fish. The ponds and streams are stuffed with brook trout, brown trout, rainbows, and some char hybrids. Little Bear Lake, where the cabins are, has thriving populations of northern pike and lake trout. Eagles and ospreys patrol the skies. With the exception of long weekends, anglers are relatively scarce.

The forests and muskeg areas harbour populations of bear, lynx, wolf, moose, elk, otter, and the occasional cougar. Even if you've retired long ago from hunting (as I have) and hate fly-fishing (as I do not), you could not help but be taken by the eskers and gemlike ponds and clear amber creeks. And the bears. Did I mention the bears?

Did Kever and I want to retreat to Dulcie Hill's cabin for the rest of our active lives, write books and paint pictures, and fly-fish in the evenings? Did we want to encounter wildlife on the margins of this community? Did we want to buy Dulcie Hill's place, no questions asked? Yer damn rights.

When we were shown inside by one of Dulcie's neighbours, we found the shack cheerless and chilly. Even the mice seemed to have abandoned it. We went for a walk, our discussion conducted in whispers. We considered the amount of work it would require to dismantle the shack and build a cabin, the money it would cost for lumber and expertise, and the commitment it would exact from us. We weren't trying to convince each other; we were probably trying to convince ourselves. But it didn't take long.

Surely there is nothing unusual about a middle-aged couple buying or building a cabin for recreational purposes. For some Canadians, it is a fundamental rite of passage. But it was unusual for us: two inexperienced klutzes who did not even own a workshop were about to erect a small house where people could sleep, cook, wash, entertain, host gatherings, work, and live. Kever is an artist, so at least she had built frames for her pictures. I had not built anything since my industrial arts class in grade nine when I was thirteen years old. My project was a graduated stick with a hole in it. The stick was used for holding up windows. I don't remember what the hole was for.

Next spring, in May 1998, Kever drove up to Little Bear with a wrecking crew. It was composed of our son Will, Kever's friend Daphne Kotzer, and her son Gavin. The theory was that even if young people were not rigorously trained in the industrial arts, they were good at wrecking things. The shack would be dismantled, all but the roof, the frame and a bit of shiplap. And so the work began.

Over the winter we had evolved a plan. We would approach all the handy people we knew and beg them to help us build a cabin. Sometimes they would get involved with the actual work; sometimes they would teach us how to do it. We would attempt to care for them, spoil them, take them fishing, and in future, lend our cabin to them when they wanted a northern vacation. In other words, we would exploit them as gently as we could.

Once Kever's crew had completed the dismantling, we called on our friend Rod MacPherson, who owned all the necessary tools and had worked with small crews to build several houses. He got us started doing the exterior of the cabin, stapling on the Tyvek, banging on the log siding, and putting in brand new bats of insulation. Rod worked fast and cheerfully and astonished us with his know-how. He showed us where to shop for bargains, helped us put in the windows and doors, and became the first of our gurus up north. By the fall, we had nailed in two outside walls of siding.

Rod Scansen was also approached in 1998. Like MacPherson, he had many tools and lots of know-how. One of the jobs he did for us was sussing out the lumber we would need for the interior and instructing me where to buy it and how to have it transported up to the lake.

"Carp," he warned me, "this ain't gonna be a walk in the park."

His words returned to haunt me over and over again.

Scansen and I priced lumber in Saskatoon and Prince Albert, prices that included paying a driver to truck it up to Little Bear for us. We crunched numbers late into the night. Things were about to get very expensive.

Another carpentry guru, Ken Bindle, told us about a little sawmill a half hour south of Little Bear.

"Might save you a few dollars," he said.

At first we were skeptical. Scanson and I drove to the sawmill and talked to the owners, a Mr. Newton and one of his sons. We showed him our shopping list: siding, knotty pine for the interior, two-by-fours, and some bigger boards for ceiling beams. He gave us a quote that was less than half the price of any of the lumber dealers down south. I assumed Mr. Newton was really going to stick it to us when we asked him to deliver.

"Ah," said Mr. Newton, "just give me a hand loading up and you can drive my truck yourself. But bring it back, eh?" I could scarcely believe our good luck.

It was late October, and the temperature had been dropping all day. The clouds began rolling in with dark resolve. I did not want to haul lumber in the rain, so we hurried with the loading. By four o'clock, with two hours of daylight remaining, I was behind the wheel of Mr. Newton's old truck.

Once again, I said to Scanson, "I can't believe our luck."

"Oh, don't worry," he said. "That sky is bound to turn ugly."

This quip of Scansen's felt like a Saskatchewan moment. Optimism is not a natural fit for Saskatchewan. Every time I hear a finance minister say, *I'm pretty optimistic about this coming fiscal year*, I get nervous. Optimism belongs in Alberta, with all their expectant capitalism. Saskatchewan's version of optimism sounds like this: *Yeah, might even get a crop this year.* Saskatchewan optimism is a guarded hope close to despair.

The truck lurched onto the narrow highway and chugged north. The wind rose, the drifts of muzzy clouds began to spit and, as we climbed into the high eskers, the rain turned to snow. At first it fell in light flurries. The truck chugged up into the hills, the lumber bounced, and the wind gusted and roared. The snow intensified and came at us flat across the road, big Christmas card flakes that, seen from the inside of a warm cabin, would have been picturesque. We climbed higher in the old truck. By then the distance to our work site was about thirty kilometres, but the gain in altitude was three hundred metres. The temperature plunged, the road froze over. The old truck began to sway and slide in the wind.

At last I spotted our turnoff. I geared down, slowed to a crawl, applied the brakes, gently pumped them—and just kept on sliding up the highway. No, Dave, said the truck, let's just head up to Flin Flon.

The highway was deserted. Scanson leapt out onto the road and began hollering directions. With my heart in my mouth, I backed up while Scanson flapped his arms like a great bird. We must have been blessed that day because, at last, under Scanson's frantic influence, I was able to turn off the highway and head down the gravel road with our lumber.

In the driving snow, we began to unload the boards. By supper-time, the darkness had fallen, but we continued to trundle the boards out of the truck and stack them inside the cabin. We stopped once to gobble a chocolate bar. Supper would have to wait.

Scanson is a lot younger and stronger than I am, so he did the heaviest lifting.

I wiped the boards dry as he stacked them. By seven-thirty, it was so dark that we had to shine Mr. Newton's headlights through our window and light candles inside.

In spite of the growing cold, we were sweating. At last, hungry and tired, we finished the job and locked up the cabin. We jumped into Mr. Newton's truck and drove back south through the storm. The truck warmed up, and without our big load, the brakes kind of worked. After dropping off the truck, we drove my car back up to Little Bear. Just as the snow began to obscure our vision by wandering and snaking across the road, we arrived at our lodgings. We made a quick supper and collapsed into our bunks.

That was it for the year. Come spring, all the new lumber would be waiting for us to whack it into place.

And a bonus for our hard work. The next morning, as we were approaching the highway to head home, I spotted a wolf.

In the spring of 1999, we returned north, determined to start work on the plumbing. Thus began the Northern Septic Tank Challenge. It meant hiring a contractor to supply the tank, a crew to dig the pit and bury the tank, and a plumber to install the pipes for the bathroom and kitchen. We decided that a system to pump in water from the lake was probably more trouble than it was worth. We would keep it simple, fetch our drinking water from the community well, and haul water by pail from the lake for washing.

We approached our northern neighbour Werner Bauer to be our plumber and, as it turned out, our counsellor. Werner was a sturdy, gruff, gregarious ex-fireman from Saskatoon who had learned a lot about life working on the oil rigs. At this time, he did only construction jobs and, with his wife Joan, stayed up at Little Bear for most of the year.

The first thing Werner wanted me to do was dig a ten-foot trench under the cabin so that he could assemble the pipes. Werner had nothing to do with the work on the septic tank, but he lined up a man to dig the pit and got things moving. I dug the trench. The big pit was dug with a backhoe, and Werner installed the pipes. But for some reason, when the septic tank was in the pit and hooked up, it started to leak. No problem, Werner told us.

"The fella's going to replace the tank. Carry on and we'll keep you posted."

Emergencies elsewhere forced me to abandon work on the site for much of 1999, but Kever brought up more voluntary crews. They came from every corner of Saskatchewan, and they will live a long time in our hearts. Judith Wright for insulation and general labour. Her five-year-old son Liam for demolition. Liam and his young friend Emmett for scraping old paint. Jane Laxdal for staining. Isobel Findlay and Alison Calder for (yuk) tearing out old insulation. Holly Borgerson Calder for insulation and staining. Bill Robertson for nailing siding and providing several grouse for supper. His son Jesse for demolition. Len Findlay for loading, hauling, and banging. Jill Robinson and Lynn Shuya, cooking for the crew. Robert Clark, sawing lumber, hauling away the remnants of Dulcie Hill's home, and all around good advice. Bob Calder for putting on the siding, banging nails into the plywood deck, and for lending us his cabin to stay in while the work was going on. Warren Cariou for siding nailed way up the ladder. Steve Smith and Clint Hunker for nailing inside knotty pine. Barb Elsasser for hauling junk away, and Doug Elsasser for working the ladders and nailing our walls into place. Andrew Taylor for insulation work and siding. Kenneth Calder and son Robert Calder Junior for deck nailing. Ken Bindle and Mac Clarke for wiring our cabin, and Ken Bindle again for nailing beams. My brother Pete Carpenter for stapling poly outside in a freezing wind.

When the snow returned in late October 1999, we had to return to civilian life, but thanks to Kever and our crews, we had a cabin that was half done. In November, Werner phoned me long distance.

"She's leakin'," he said.

He didn't have to explain who she was. For mysterious reasons, the septic tank was still not functioning. A young man from the crew had tried to fix the leak by digging down to the elbow, where the tank joins up with the pipes, detaching the elbow, cleaning and drying it with a hair drier, and joining the assembly with a massive amount of tar. He had gone away confident that the leak was a thing of the past, but ground water was still getting into our tank. It seemed we had the wrong elbow and gasket for the tank. Werner listened patiently while I bemoaned my outcast fate.

"You gotta remember, Dave, that north of the Torch things move real slow."

I nodded my understanding into the receiver. Werner Bauer's words seemed to sum up the rhythms of an entire northern community.

I tried to explain to Kever why our septic tank still did not work.

"So," she surmised, "when we return in the spring we still have no toilet."

"Right."

"The neighbours will see us coming and slam their doors."

"Right," I said.

"We'll have to hold it in till we get up to the store or hike off into the bushes."

"You have to realize, Kever, that north of the Torch things move real slow."

She gave me a look that wives flash at their husbands from time to time. This look means: *Really*, shouted, followed by both a question mark and an exclamation mark. That night, she brought up a lovely urn from our basement. It was her mother's ancient chamber pot.

In the spring of 2000, Bob Calder and I went into the woods above the lake in search of a dead tree to serve as the central beam for the living room. Ken Bindle, our guiding light of carpentry at that time, had given us specific orders: it must be four inches in diameter, and it must look nice when the bark is scraped away. North of the Torch, things might tend to move slowly, but not when Bindle was around.

Calder and I headed for a burn area where young pine and spruce were starting to regenerate and the burnt trees towered black above them, leaning at weird angles. Some trees had escaped destruction from the great fire that had descended on Little Bear a few years before, but none was the right size. We moved along, measuring and scraping bark away, until we found a black spruce just the right size. We took turns chopping until the tree came down. We sawed off the top at four inches in diameter, then took off the bottom and threw the tree into the truck. Down at the work site, we peeled away the bark and beheld a beautiful network of dark vermiculations in the light brown wood. The worms were long gone but they had left behind the intricate designs of their pathways.

Bindle and Kever came out to admire our log. It would stand from floor to ceiling in the middle of our living area, and all our friends could admire the loops and scrolls left behind by the worms as though they had taken their designs from a higher power. Bindle conducted the raising of the log and, with some ceremony, we hammered it to the ceiling beams. *Raise high the roof beam, Carpenter. This shack is going to become a cabin.*

Somehow, over the winter, something changed in Kever and me. The mental blocks to doing carpentry had fallen away. When we returned to Little Bear that spring, our lessons all came back. The more knotty pine siding we nailed on, the smaller the pile of lumber in the centre of our living area became. Often Kever would work outside, planting trees around the yard, and then she would come inside to do the finer work on boards that needed to be fitted and tucked into the tops of the walls.

The inside work began to absorb us, and we became less reliant on our handy friends for their labour and instructions. I got obsessed with finishing the knotty pine inside. Each morning I would gulp down my breakfast and dash off to the work site to bang boards. Spring melted into summer, and summer baked into fall. By October, we were ready for the cabinets to be hammered in, the old chimney to be replaced, and our newly acquired wood heating stove to be installed.

So we went to the man who, in a sense, started it all, David Baxter. We had bartered with his brother, George, for a small but durable wood stove that was just right for our little cabin. Later, we got David to help us with the building of a new deck and a screened-in porch. As always, I would be his helper and he the patient instructor. He would say things like, "Help me shim these rafters, will ya," or, "Find the joist over there and measure from the stud," and I would say "Wha," and Baxter would explain it to me in words that a ten-year-old could understand. After a while, I improved at banging things together.

One night in the early spring of 2001, we got a call in Saskatoon from that other happy handyman–guru, Werner Bauer. We'd been planning to get up north to finish our work on the cabin. We were sounding downright cocky about our progress of the previous fall. We had a wood stove, new siding, a new interior, and a new toilet donated by Ken Bindle.

Werner said, "Dave, she's leakin' again."

A man with a cabin is a wondrous thing, but a man without a toilet is nothing.

He must inveigle his way into the homes of unsuspecting neighbours in order to use their facilities. He has to try different strategies each morning or they will be on to him. He must switch neighbours in order to change his pattern. He will try the store once in a while, perhaps even try the nearest motel fifteen kilometres away. Whatever pretense he uses, he must eventually say, "Mind if I use your can?" Timing is crucial.

On this particular week, one of our neighbours, Andy Beaulac, and his friend, Jerry Shuya, came into the picture. Andy provided us with a new tank and the new fixtures, Jerry with the know-how. But they would need me and son Will for grunt work. On a warm day at the end of June, we gathered to await the arrival of the backhoe for what everyone at Little Bear would refer to as The Fourth Great Excavation. I am not known up here for my books or for my angling wizardry; I am known for my septic tank.

Just as the backhoe arrived at the rear of our lot, neighbours from all over the settlement began to gather. First, the backhoe man had to drain off the excess water from our tank, and for this he attached an ancient hose to a pump and cranked it up. Perhaps the hose was too old to do the job. By now, it was more duct tape than rubber. When the water from my tank flowed into the hose, it exploded all over the yard, and because I was manning the hose, I got sprayed with more coliform than flies in a backhouse. Until he has been sprayed by his own effluent, does a man truly know his own smell? The water was so foul that the good neighbours felt compelled to back away, and some have never returned.

The man at the pump was Daniel, a big strapping boy of sixteen and very gifted at making the backhoe do his bidding. With its insatiable iron maw, gouging into the earth around our tank, it looked like *Tyrannosaurus rex*. But I was surprised by the delicacy with which the big machine deposited the soil around the hole. As the backhoe moved away from the worksite, I moved closer and beheld a gaping pit in which Will and I would do our digging. When Daniel's backhoe lumbered down the road to get gravel, Will and I descended into the pit. Our job was to dig down to the leaking elbow so that Jerry Shuya could remove it and replace it with the one that would fit properly. For Will and me, this meant wallowing around in man-eating gumbo for several hours. By noon, Will and I knew that we were in for a long day. Kever brought beer and sandwiches, and we sat in the shade for a while to rest. We climbed back down into the pit for the last bit of prepping work ahead of Jerry Shuya's refitting job for the new elbow. No one wanted to work at the edge of the tank. The methane was enough to curl my hair—and I'm bald. But Jerry seemed to have more determination than all of us put together, so as he did the prying and fitting, we kept shoveling the mud and sand away from the edge of the pit. Will got stuck in a bad wallow and he simply could not dislodge his right leg.

"Whatever you do, Will," I cautioned, "do not abandon your rubber boot."

I must have given him the wrong idea. He drew his foot out of the boot and lurched away. But he couldn't climb out of the pit without his boot, so with the greatest reluctance, he returned to the boot, reinserted his foot, and began to tug once more. Poor young man, nothing was working for him, and the rest of us were too absorbed in our task to come and help.

"Let's just forget the whole thing," Will moaned. "Let's go back to outhouses."

Maybe Dulcie Hill had been right all along.

At that moment, Kever came over and scrutinized us. I recall that she was shaking her head. We must have looked like throwbacks, half men, half warthogs, covered in gumbo and grunting our disapproval to one another. Kever returned with a sheet of plywood and an old wooden ladder, and soon, with both of his boots on, Will was climbing up into the world of light and warm beds and cups of tea.

When a guy is in dire straits, who does he really need? His mother, nine times out of ten.

We sealed the tank and Daniel dumped gravel down the hole to protect it from the seepage of the ground water. Very skillfully, Daniel filled in the pit with gobs of gumbo, and then we all had a beer in the sunlight. Will was smiling. Jerry Shuya was smiling. Andy was smiling. I was smiling. The neighbours in our tiny settlement would at last have something else to talk about.

In September 2001, when David Baxter finished his labours on our screened-in porch, all we had left to do was fix the old roof. One of the jobs was shingling. The roof was covered in ancient asphalt shingles put there by Mrs. Hill and an old fellow who had kept company with her. Apparently he was blind, so Dulcie would place each shingle before him and he would nail it. As the story goes, the two began drinking up on the roof and, as night fell, the shingling continued and so did the drinking, until the job was done.

I hadn't paid much attention to this tale until I joined Jerry Shuya on top of the cabin. It was an ancient roof with a large dip in the middle. It had a resigned look. Some of the shingles came off with almost no effort. As it turned out, these were the ones Dulcie's friend had not quite managed to nail down. Other shingles had to be assaulted, shredded and pried. They had been nailed within an inch of their lives. Dulcie and her old friend had used six different kinds of nails to do the job. You can never know a person until you've pulled her shingles.

And here, next to a pail full of Dulcie's old nails, I end my tale. I've just been staring up at Jerry Shuya's new roof, admiring David Baxter's new porch, checking out Kever's staining of the logs, checking out the doors and windows. And remembering. Such a time we had. So many meals shared after work with friends and neighbours. So many trials, so many gurus, so much grunting.

Tonight, Kever and I are alone in the cabin (yes, it's now a bona fide cabin), and the sun is setting over Little Bear Lake. Pink-bellied clouds are scudding through a delft-blue sky. The geese are a mile high, barking out their wacky colloquies. These goose calls are coming through the screen of the last window that Rod MacPherson installed. The Baxter stove is glowing with the embers from the wood we gathered. Our axe, a house-warming present from the Calders, leans from the big wormwood post that Bindle helped us to install. Every square foot in this cabin reminds me of the excellent people who built it.

The land outside our cabin had been severely disturbed by our construction crews. Kever was dreaming of the trees and bushes she would plant, how they would give us shade in the hot summers and absorb carbon dioxide. I was dreaming of the day when our first bear might arrive, our first rabbits, our first deer, our first lynx. This in turn reminded me of another cabin from a long time ago, where I encountered my first monster.

CHAPTER 18

My First Monster

*W*hen I was eight years old, we rented a summer cabin at Kapasiwin Beach on Lake Wabamun, an hour's drive west of Edmonton. It was so old, musty, and damp that it seemed more like the corpse of a cabin than a real cabin. Its log footings were no doubt in deep decay, because with each year the cabin settled lower and lower into the ground. We loved it. The cabin slouched on a rise above the lake so close to the beach that we could make it down to the water in under one minute.

I had two weeks to figure out how to catch a fish, but the days flew by and I still hadn't managed to get one strike. Soon I would have to go back to the city and forget about fishing for another year. I asked Bobby LeClaire where I could catch one. LeClaire was several years older than me. He spoke with authority about speed boats, shooting rabbits, boxing, horse racing, football, and girls. I wasn't interested in any of that. I was aching to catch a fish.

He told me to try the raft in the evening.

"Later the better," he said.

The raft was anchored in deep water, enticingly close to the public pier. I told Bobby that our family didn't have a proper boat.

"You can swim, right?"

Yes, I could swim, but swimming with a fishing rod in tow seemed a bit of a challenge. LeClaire walked me out to the end of the long public pier. The raft was a stationary old hulk, and when the wind was up it seemed to strain on its anchor towards the eastern shore. But like me, it never got anywhere. The distance to the raft from where we stood was probably no more than a hundred feet, but the water was deep.

"Get someone to row you out there," he said. "You want fish, that's where you go."

As he strode away, I asked him how I would get back to shore.

"Figure it out," Bobby said in closing. He said that a lot.

That evening I was alone on the pier in my bathing suit with my father's old handline. The line was dark green and very thick, and it was wound like carded wool between two carved notches on a piece of wood. To this line I had attached a big spoon known as a red devil, its paint scratched by the teeth of many a pike. At my feet was an inflated inner tube—all this because I had figured it out.

My brother was somewhere down the lake. My over-protective father and my over-protective mother were up in our rented cabin, under the impression that I was cavorting with my brother and his older friends. I remember this moment as a determined and fearless one, but not necessarily a courageous one. Around my neck was a Boy Scout whistle that my father insisted I wear any time I played outside in the woods at night. *In case you get lost out there*, he said. *In case you run into trouble.* I wore the whistle under protest, and I was determined never to use it.

The water felt cold but the evening was warm, so I donned the inflated inner tube and thrashed and kicked my way out to the raft. As I unwound the cord from the spindle, I heard an owl hooting and the rise and fall of chorusing frogs. A loon cried and, further off, another shrieked back lunacies at the coming night. Soaking wet, I faced the sunset and began to swing the big lure like a lariat around my head. As the line grew longer it uncoiled at my feet, my body twisting to widen the orbit of the lure. I released it in a soaring arc, and it plunged into the water. I waited for the spoon to sink and brought it in slowly, hand over hand.

My memory of this first cast of the evening is a golden one, displaying my skills in this rudimentary exercise, but I doubt it was that skillful. I was too young and too excited to be skillful. And wouldn't my much-loathed whistle on its cord have gotten in the way? Did I toss the whistle over my shoulder to hang down my back?

I remember the sensation of something watching me on the raft. I was wondering what that creature might look like, when a fish grabbed my spoon, a small pike that came in spiraling feebly to the raft. I unhooked the fish and it slimed out of my grip back into the water. It went belly up on the surface then righted itself and darted away. I swung my handline around once again and sent it into the sunset. I hauled in the line, coiling it in loops at my feet, anchoring the spindle with my foot. My small pike swam back near the surface as though it were lost.

I climbed onto the diving board to make a longer cast, and this time I waited longer for the spoon to sink. I was alone and doing all this in the fading light without my big brother and my parents, which somehow turned this adventure into a heroic quest. The stricken fish I'd caught was still swimming in circles when suddenly the water beneath it curled into a whirlpool, and my fish disappeared.

My god.

When my line was about halfway in, something nudged it, not a strike, more like a slap, and my arms flinched as though whatever was watching me had made a grab at my goose-pimpled flesh. I spotted my lure as it wobbled up from the depths. A blackness appeared in the dark water, as though something shapeless was lurking beneath my lure. A black hole about the size of a man's head came up towards my wobbling lure, and surrounding this hole, an open set of jaws, a huge open maw.

I gasped. A thing as big as I was, a green long thing with eyes wide and cold, drifted after my spoon.

I yanked my spoon out of the water.

The fish glided past, its tail swept right out of the lake and the water erupted with a smack. The monster fish was hovering just beneath the surface. It turned, very slowly, tilted its body to look up and faced me. It seemed to be grinning. I was fixed in place by its gaze, frozen bird to ancient serpent. Without moving a fin, the great fish sank down into the depths of the lake.

The thrill of that moment had turned to fear. I had heard from my father about wolves up north, about cougars in the foothills and grizzlies in the mountains, black bears here and there, and polar bears away up north, and I loved to hear him talk about them because they were scary and dangerous and they could eat you up. But in my own small world, which included Lake Wabamun and our rented cabin and the city where we lived, I never thought I would engage with a monster.

It was getting dark. I was shivering and I had to get home. This meant packing up my handline, getting back into my inflated inner tube, dangling my legs in the water inhabited by the grinning pike, and thrashing my way to the pier.

No. There had to be limits as to how heroic I was prepared to be. I climbed back onto the diving board and faced the shore. I stuck the despised whistle into my mouth and blew it as long and as loud as my lungs would allow.

EPILOGUE

The Numen*

I seem to have a thing for predatory animals. My journals are full of them. Some of these creatures—such as spiders, snakes, wolves, cougars, and bears—can give us nightmares. Some are the stuff of phobias, including my own. Like the beasts of myth and legend, they frighten us. They have even been known, infrequently, to attack us. Bears huff, cougars shriek, wolves howl, rattlers buzz, and spiders scuttle through some of our scariest dreams and fantasies. In this sense, they *are* the beasts of myth and legend. Perhaps when the most magnificent of these creatures are completely extinguished and their wild habitat domesticated, we will begin to revere them in

---

* A numen is a local or presiding deity or spirit. Among ancient and Indigenous peoples, the numen sometimes took on the shape of a large carnivore. A numinous experience is not just a scary encounter, but an awe-inspiring one with a divinity. It's said to be more of a spiritual encounter. The best modern version of this experience that I can think of is recounted in Margaret Atwood's novel, *Surfacing*.

that safe way that some of us revere *Tyrannosaurus rex*. Defending these living creatures from encroachment and slaughter might seem like an uphill battle, but defend them we must.

To do this, we need to protect the world they live in—which leads me to the problems and challenges of global warming. We have managed to overpopulate our planet to such an extent that we strain our resources to satisfy our growing needs for food, housing, and energy. Many of these resources, like fossil fuels, are non-renewable, and the extractive raid that we are conducting, with its great polluting masses of exhaust, hits hard at our ever-decreasing wilderness.

David Attenborough (*A Life on our Planet*) recommends that we rewild the planet, replacing the tame with the wild wherever possible. A local initiative that appeals to me is planting more trees in public places, on private lots, on rural properties, or in logged-out forests. If this initiative could be implemented on a really large scale in the coming decades, forests could rise from their ashes and from clear-cuts, and we might once again re-engage with an abundance of wild animals, including the dangerous, endangered ones—the apex carnivores—that we have been destroying for so long.

You who have read these pages know that apex predators are the animals that fascinate me most of all, with their strength, their speed, their cunning, and their unutterable beauty. Most of them face greater perils than the creatures they hunt to survive. The odds against their survival into adulthood are huge compared to anything we humans face. All over North America, indeed all over the world, the largest of these predators are moving ever closer to extinction because we fear them, or at the very least, because we find them inconvenient. We have turned them into commodities. We want their pelts, their fins, their organs, their claws, and their blubber, and we want their living bodies alive for our zoos, marinas and animal shows. We want to take over their territory to turn their wild habitats into industrial sites, ski lodges, theme parks, and suburbs. Once we've hunted and poisoned them into oblivion, or run them over with our vehicles, we will happily continue to name streets, sports franchises, motels, cars, and luxury trailers after them.

We humans are the driving force in what many global observers are calling the sixth extinction. An extinction event refers to a sudden cataclysm that compromises Earth's biodiversity and drastically reduces the numbers of multicellular organisms. The rate of extinction then exceeds the rate of new species evolving. The first of these was the Ordovician-Silurian extinction 444 million years ago (in which small marine organisms, trilobites, corals, and clam-like brachiopods were destroyed). The second event was the late Devonian extinction, occurring from 383 million to 359 million years ago (tropical marine specimens, placoderms, larger trilobites, and more varieties of coral). The third event was the big one, the Permian-Triassic extinction 252 million years ago that destroyed a huge range of species (amphibians, apex marine predators, and many other vertebrates). The fourth one was the Triassic-Jurassic extinction 201 million years ago (fish such as the conodonts, reptiles, and other vertebrates). Dinosaurs survived the fourth extinction but were erased by the fifth one: the Cretaceous-Paleogene event 66 million years ago (dinosaurs, ammonites, mollusks, other animals, and plants).

Scientists usually date the sixth phase, the Holocene extinction, as starting when humans first gathered in agricultural settlements: the advent of what we like to call civilization, from ten thousand years ago till the present day.

With the massive increase in human population, the increase in resource development, the acceleration of fossil fuel consumption, the release of greenhouse gases, and the resultant change in the climate, species extinctions have risen drastically. This tragic spiral of wild animal mortality began with humans carving up and then destroying the animals' habitats. As wilderness has become more accessible to vehicles, trophy hunters and poachers have extirpated local fauna, including the last of the apex predators. We are at present losing the snow leopards and Amur tigers. We are closing in on lions, orcas, polar bears, and our North American cougars.

This dilemma begs the question of what humans will become once they have swarmed over all the wilderness and killed off all the apex predators—the ones with the power to frighten us. Our tolerance for these creatures is rarely as steadfast as our fear. Think of the moment when you wander into a spiderweb and turn into a karate master, or when you awaken in your tent to the sound of heavy footpads and snuffling. In our dreams, it's our imagination that takes over the narrative, and in the real forest, when our flashlight gets misplaced, say, our imagination steps in and suggests a dreadful scenario, prompting a foolish decision. *Exterminate the brutes!*

Awakening from the terrors of night to the prosaic light of day, we tend to lose our fears and greet the morning with a yawn. This is the right frame of mind to meditate on the magnificence of carnivores.

For early human civilizations, bears, lions, wolves, alligators, and the other apex predators were treated as numena, presiding deities. Imagine encountering a grizzly at close quarters on an alpine meadow. Your first impulse might be to run—always a mistake in grizzly territory. The hair at the back of your neck might rise up and your legs begin to shake. In what we like to call primitive times, this response would have included more than just fear. There would also have been awe at beholding the size and the enormous strength of the deity, the numen that a human person must respect in order to survive in the wilderness.

This is what we mean when we talk about a numinous experience. You don't run away from the numen, but you might reach for your pepper spray and back away respectfully. Some suggest that you talk to the bear, so that what begins in fear ends in détente and perhaps even reverence.

When we've wiped out all the grizzlies, who will inherit their power? The one with the high-powered rifle and scope? The guy with the chainsaw? The developer? The smiling realtor? The corporation that monetizes old-growth forests? If these become our presiding deities, our planet is in even more trouble than we can imagine.

When I first began my work on this book, I was not thinking about food chains, or the wild carnivore's role in pest control, or anything else related to predator ecology. I was reading through my accumulation of field notes in order to summon memories of snakes, cougars, wolves, bears, and other animals. If I was thinking about anything at all in the abstract, the word would be magnificence. These animals and their habitats need to be defended from destruction because they are magnificent. The dragonflies hawking for horseflies in the bright light of summer. The tiny weasel, rushing through tunnels beneath the snowdrifts, looking for mice. The grizzly, fattened for hibernation, rising up from the rockslides like a sumo wrestler awaiting combat. The rattlesnake weaving in the night, winding through the cactus and over the desert floor. The phantom cougar, unseen but all-seeing, drifting low through the salal shrubs. Like the regions they inhabit, these beasts are all magnificent.

Their habitats are also magnificent. As James Snider, a scientist with the World Wildlife Fund in Canada, reported, "We can't simply be taking an approach to protected areas that is separate from how we're tackling climate change, that is separate from how we're trying to recover our species at risk. They have to be deeply integrated." I love the depth of commitment in this statement.

🐍

I began this book with an excerpt from *Sapiens* by Yuval Noah Harari. Sometimes he grumbles at us, including the most avid of his readers, like a disapproving god. At the end of *Sapiens*, contemplating the entire sad chronicle of human history, he fires a final salvo at our species, implying that the more powerful we have become, the less inclined we are to use this power responsibly. We are no longer accountable for what we do, and in consequence, "we are wreaking havoc on our fellow animals and on the surrounding ecosystem" for selfish motives such as greater recreation or greater comfort. Much as I believe that Harari's indictment is justified, it need not be taken as the final word on humanity. We don't have to accept our traditional roles as poachers, jet-set trophy hunters, collectors, and traders of rare species, destroyers of wild habitat, destroyers of ocean ecology, and so on. We don't have to slouch away from Harari's condemnation of human destruction and moral complacency and resume walking down our destructive paths. We can look around our neighbourhoods, towns, and regions and commit to simple and constructive actions, many of them potentially joyful, exhilarating, and creative.

Imagine once more those trees newly planted in a clear-cut wasteland, a wood lot, a provincial park, a burnt out forest, your own backyard, or on an abandoned piece of land near your home. The trees grow and, each spring, they surge forth in leafy shades of green. Imagine the birds and animals returning to these trees.

Then imagine the rabbits as they multiply like rabbits. Our natural predators large and small will maintain the necessary ecological balance in these re-established habitats, while the forests do their work of absorbing carbon dioxide and giving off oxygen. I say this at a time when the price of timber has skyrocketed and forests are being clear-cut and burned down at an alarming rate. But, thanks in part to human initiatives, forests throughout the ravaged world have also, over the past two decades, been regenerating at an impressive rate. This regeneration will continue if we let it. If my wife can grow a micro-forest on disturbed land in the boreal region by using trees native to that region, and if our friends the carnivores give their approval to this new habitat by returning to it, we are off to a good start.

I've seen this process unfold on our own property. The animals in their precarious diminishing habitats are waiting to come home. In the meantime, while the climate scientists, biologists, naturalists, politicians, and entrepreneurs of the world figure out how to bring zero-carbon energies into our midst, just imagine what we could do locally.

Earlier in this essay, I said that predacious creatures deserve our protection because they are magnificent. But they are more than magnificent. In their own habitats, they are like lords. This is particularly true of apex predators who, in earlier tribal societies, were revered and in some cases worshipped. In his book, *Monster of God*, David Quammen studies how early and recent communities have revered the predatory animals that live in their regions. Among the Udege people and other forest people of Northeastern Russia and Manchuria, Amur tigers were venerated like gods of the forest. There is evidence that this veneration might still be going on. In the Carpathian Mountains of Eastern Romania, the brown bear is still flourishing. Occasionally a bear will kill and devour a sheep. Most of the shepherds don't use guns, and instead they fend off the bears with their sheep dogs. In Romanian lore, the brown bear is a sort of partner in the woods with shepherds and trappers, an all-powerful presence that must be befriended. As Quammen observes in *Monster of God*, the Romanian brown bear is regarded by some shepherds as "the treasure of the forest." A difficult friend to be sure, but a forest without bears is empty.

From Quammen's book we learn that the saltwater crocodile (*Crocodylus porosus*) has also maintained its totemic status among the Aboriginal peoples of Arnhem Land in Northern Australia. The Gurr-goni clan sees crocodiles as reincarnations of their ancestors. The Gumatj clan maintains that their clan originated from the crocodile. Among the clans of nearby Yolngu, there are several animal-centred clans, including the crocodile people.

Many would argue that wilderness is sacred. In the wilderness habitats where apex predators live, they too are sacred—beyond the ancient enclaves of animal worship, beyond the domains of present day Indigenous shamans and subsistence hunters who consider them as family, beyond the vast networks of informed animal lovers who fight for their conservation. These great bears, these cougars, wolves, serpents, crocodiles, orcas, leopards, lions, and tigers, can still evoke in us a numinous experience when we encounter them in their territory. I'm talking about that moment when we behold them in all their deadly strength, when we fear and revere them, that moment of awe. And if we allow their destruction, this moment of awe is lost to us.

ACKNOWLEDGEMENTS

*T*his last section is not only an acknowledgement of sources, chapter by chapter, but an extended valentine to the many writers who instructed me in all things woodsy, stealthy, furry, scaly, scary, and wondrous, with which, for years, I have been trying to get better acquainted. Much of what I have written here comes from my own experiences in the wilds and from the field notes I've scribbled in my diaries for more than five decades. Calling up these woodsy encounters can be a highly subjective process, but researching them, giving them context, and trying to articulate them is a discipline. To me, wild carnivores are like interesting but reclusive neighbours who protect their privacy. Researching this book has forced me to snoop into the private lives of creatures I've always wondered about. It's one thing to be an enchanted tourist in the woods—to love dragonflies, for example. It's quite another thing to discover the details of their life cycles, their very long larval periods under water as predacious nymphs, and the surprising brevity of their lives as sexually mature dragonflies. One reading of Hutchings and Halstead's *Dragonflies & Damselflies in the Hand* (2011) deepened my appreciation of these admirable, predatory insects.

I have a much larger indebtedness to David Quammen, whose learned, witty, cosmopolitan, science-friendly essays have drawn me further into the mysteries of the natural world. Closer to home, I'm indebted, by their books and their examples, to two activists who have fought battles unrelentingly on behalf of endangered wildlife and natural environments: Trevor Herriot and Candace Savage. If you two have a club in common, I'd like to join.

Another dedicated, eloquent, and observant nature writer, one whose essays have a pronounced literary appeal, is Craig Childs, whose narratives entice us to walk the trails and look harder. Try *The Secret Knowledge of Water* and *The Animal Dialogues* for starters.

The genesis of this book was a lunch conversation with Bruce Walsh, the former director and publisher of University of Regina Press. I told him that if I ever wrote another nonfiction book, it would have something to do with wild predators such as bears, wolves, and cougars. Bruce leapt at the suggestion, and much later, so did I.

Three of my best and meanest friends read this manuscript, chapter by chapter, and offered criticism: David Margoshes, Dwayne Brenna, and Don Kerr (recently deceased). At first, we four gathered every month in person, and later on Zoom, and somehow we managed to make our winters seem shorter. As well, Len Findlay did some helpful coaching. He, Warren Cariou, and Bob Calder read parts of this manuscript and were quite encouraging.

My editor was the renowned novelist, Fred Stenson. Until now, I had no idea what a great editor he is. I'm grateful for his awareness of nature and his knowledge of predacious animals in the wilds. And, because of his close attention to my manuscript, thousands of my best modifiers lie writhing on the cutting room floor. I almost don't miss them.

Finally, I want to acknowledge the work done by my supremely outdoorsy wife, Honor Kever, who read drafts of this manuscript and suggested corrections, and who has camped, hiked, fished, and driven the blue highways with me on many forays into nature. She is my first reader, my fellow adventurer, and my ongoing source of inspiration.

NOTES AND SOURCES
BY CHAPTER

Introduction
A Consideration of Creatures with Fangs, Claws, and Other Pointy Things

Pages 4–5 In his book, *Monster of God: The Man-Eating Predator in the Jungles of History and the Mind* (New York: W. W. Norton and Company, 2003), pages 410 and 414, David Quammen predicts a probable end to apex predators in the wild (lions, tigers, bears, crocodiles, wolves, and constrictors) towards the middle of the next century. I take this observation more as a warning than a certainty.

Chapter 1
The Bad Bug

Pages 9–14 My first encounter with a story about mosquitoes as predatory creatures was "Mosquito" by Craig Childs, *The Animal Dialogues* (New York: Little, Brown and Company, 2009 paperback edition). Among his other books is *The Secret Knowledge of Water* (New York: Little, Brown and Company, 2000). Both books are page turners, filled with revelations about nature, and basic reading for armchair as well as scuffed-boot naturalists. My most edifying introduction to the mosquito was David Quammen's essay, "Sympathy for the Devil" in *Natural Acts* (New York: W. W. Norton & Company, Inc., 2008). Two of the most helpful websites about the global dangers of mosquito-borne viruses were from the Public Health Agency of Canada and the Government of Saskatchewan health site.

Page 12 News of the release of genetically altered male mosquitoes into the Florida Keys comes from <theguardian.com> April 28, 2021.

Page 12 Timothy Winegard, *The Mosquito: A Human History of our Greatest Predator* (Penguin Random House, 2019).

Chapter 2
The Good Bug
Pages 15–19 I wrote an early draft of "The Good Bug" in the summer of 2011 and put it in the drawer. Several years later, I pulled out the story and began doing research on dragonflies. Gordon Hutchings and David Halstead's book, *Dragonflies & Damselflies in the Hand* (Regina: Nature Saskatchewan Publications, 2011) was very enlightening, as were their photographs. The book was written by entomologists but is accessible to general readers. My mosquito essay was first published in *Prairies North*, Summer, 2020, pages 17–19.

Chapter 3
Itsy-Bitsy Phobia
Pages 22–23 Paul Hillyard, *The Private Life of Spiders* (Princeton, New Jersey: Princeton University Press, 2011), pages 136–37.

Page 23 The more research done by arachnid scientists, the greater is the number of identified species of spiders. In the year 2021, Marcus Buehler, a research professor at the Massachusetts Institute of Technology, has upped this number into the neighbourhood of forty-seven thousand species.

Page 24 On the subject of wandering spiders in South America, Don Buckle, a spider expert in Saskatoon, was very helpful. He introduced me to a number of academic tomes, the most illuminating of which were Wolfgang Bucherl, "Biology and Venoms of the Most Important South American Spiders of the Genera *Phoneutria, Loxosceles, Lycosa* and *Latrodectus*," *American Zoologist* Vol. 9, pages 157–59, 1969; and especially, Sylvia Lucas, "Spiders in Brazil," *Toxicon*, Volume 26, pages 759–72, 1988.

Pages 24–25 A very handy reference book for spider enthusiasts in North America, and especially in Canada, is John and Kathleen Hancock's *Spiders of Western Canada* (Vancouver: Lone Pine, 2016). They were especially helpful to me in their discussion of venomous varieties such as black widows and brown recluses (violin spiders). John Hancock's illustrations are very precise. I also consulted Herb and Lorna Levi's Golden Guide handbook, *Spiders and their Kin* (1990 edition). They are knowledgeable but disconcertingly old school. For example, the best way to collect spiders is to kill them first. For statistics on fatalities from black widow and brown recluse bites, I googled Schenone and Suarez, "Arthropod Venoms," in Sergio Bettini (ed.), *Handbook of Experimental Pharmacology* (Berlin: Springer Verlag, 1978).

Page 26 Information about the sounds produced and received by spiders and about the strength of spiderwebs comes from several sources, but the most current is Markus Buehler's recent work, summarized in an interview. See "Spinning some Tunes,"

Saskatoon StarPhoenix, Saturday, April 17, 2021, section B, page 6. For a fuller account, google Buehler's work on scitechdaily.com.

Chapter 4
Lo, the Serpent

Page 29 Harry Greene in Richard Louv, *Our Wild Calling: How connecting with animals can transform our lives—and save theirs* (Chapell Hill: Algonquin Books, 2019), page 52.

Page 36 Robert L. Smith, *Venomous Animals of Arizona* (Tucson: University of Arizona Press, 1989 edition). Black and white drawings are by Joel Floyd. Of all the resource books, guidebooks, and brochures that I consulted on this trip, Smith's volume was by far the best. He was particularly informative on rattlesnake and arthropod physiology. There is something in here for zoologists and hobbyists alike.

For identifying species of rattlesnake, I used Dick and Sharon Nelson's field guide to *Snakes of Arizona* (Phoenix: Primer Publishers, 1985).

Pages 40–41 Austin Stevens, *Snakemaster: Wildlife Adventures with the World's Most Dangerous Reptiles* (New York: Skyhorse Publishing, 2019).

Pages 41–42 G.A. Bradshaw, *Carnivore Minds* (New Haven: Yale University Press, 2017), pages 164–66.

Page 42 Richard Louv, *Our Wild Calling: How connecting with animals can transform our lives—and save theirs* (Chapel Hill: Algonquin Books, 2019), pages 48–52.

Page 43 My envenomation statistics come primarily from sciencedaily.com and from "Venomous Snakebites in Canada," an article posted on wemjournal.org.

Chapter 5
Chuga-rum, Chuga-rum

Pages 45–46 I would describe the evolution of the crocodile in the same fashion as I have the alligator, of course, but crocodiles are extremely scarce on this continent and I've never seen one in the wilds.

Pages 45–47 Many of the more recondite details on the evolution of alligators were googled from several sources, including ThoughtCo. For some details on the evolution of frogs, see the article by Pearl Tesler, "The Amazing Adaptable Frog," on the Exploratorium website.

Chapter 6
Popping Weasels

Pages 52–53 Mark Elbroch and Kurt Rinehart, *Behavior of North American Mammals* (New York: Houghton Mifflin Harcourt Publishing Company; Peterson Reference Guide, 2011), pages 170–76.

Page 52 On weasel anatomy and acute night vision, see "13 Things You Never Knew about Weasels," in countrylife.co.uk/nature.

Page 52 By rabbits I mean hares. I sometimes prefer the language I grew up with to the language urged upon us by the taxonomists.

Chapter 7
Saving the Cutthroat at McArthur Lake

Page 61 Cutthroat trout up around Lake O'Hara and McArthur Lake usually do their spawning between one and three months before the brook trout spawn. This leaves the McArthur cutthroat eggs and fry vulnerable to brook trout invasions throughout the warmer months. Brook trout are an exotic species for this region. They spawn in the autumn when other trout species have begun to slow down and lose their summer appetites.

For an update on saving the cutthroat (in this case, the westslope cutthroat), see Brad Stitt's impressive report on how his crew removes the brook trout and prepares the habitat for the native cutthroat to reoccupy their lakes and streams.

Google: Brad Stitt westslope cutthroat trout conservation.

Chapter 8
Call Me Ahab

Page 67 Note to anglers: My mention of Russia's brown trout streams was penned just before their invasion of Ukraine. Your travel plans might need adjusting.

Page 67 One of the keys to healthier brown trout populations in Europe and the British Isles is the dismantling of defunct dams. There are about one hundred and fifty thousand of these dams, and in the past two decades about five thousand have come down all over Europe. This is also true for fishing streams in North America and elsewhere. From the January 28, 2022, article cbc.ca/radio/asithappens/as-it-happens-the-Monday-edition.

Page 68 The enterprising anglers in question were Bill Robertson (in a stream) and Warren Cariou (on a lake).

Page 68 "The whole gang of us," as far as I can remember, amounts to twelve brown trout zealots.

Page 69 The use of barbless hooks for the purpose of releasing trout unharmed is most often done by fly fishers. Spin fishers, gang trollers and bait jiggers are not usually equipped to do catch-and-release fishing.

Chapter 9
Curiosity

Page 72 For information on river otters and their relationships with beavers, see Elbroch and Rinehart, *Behaviour of North American Mammals*, page 158.

Chapter 10
Interrogating the Sphynx

Pages 79–80 To check information on lynxes, I consulted both the canadiangeographic.ca and bigcatrescue.org websites. These two sources give concise facts on this enigmatic animal.

Chapter 11
Nocturnal Chorales

Page 84 For updates on coyote populations throughout North America, go to rainforestalliance.org.

Page 84 For average weight of coyotes, see Ian Sheldon and Tamara Hartson, *Animal Tracks of British Columbia* (Edmonton: Lone Pine Publishing, 1999), page 40.

Page 85 On the varieties of coyote vocal utterances, see Philip Lehner and Major Bodicker, "Making sense of coyote vocalizations," outdoornews.com, November 16, 2016.

Page 87 Statistics on deaths caused by coyotes can be googled using the search terms "fatalities from coyotes in North America." Information on the two deaths in North America can be accessed on Wikipedia. Figures cited on the massive annual slaughter of coyotes every year are from therainforestsite.greatergood.com.

Pages 87–88 The information on coyotes harassing people in Canada comes from surveys done by the University of Calgary and from *The Vancouver Sun*, January 23, 2021, page 3A. A recent rash of coyote attacks in Calgary, yet to be reported on in any detail, may well echo the problems reported in Vancouver.

Page 88 Some of the details on coyote predation in Vancouver are from *Quirks & Quarks*, CBC Radio 1, April 10, 2021.

Chapter 12
Going Forth to Multiply

Page 89 Questions sometimes arise as to the genetic and evolutionary connections between bears and pigs. There are no such connections. Bears come from the *Ursidae* family and pigs from the *Suidae* family.

Pages 89–96 Details on the history, ecology, diet, and management of feral hogs can be perused and updated on many websites. Here are some helpful examples: the Canadian Wildlife Service website, the animals.mom.com website, and especially John C. Kinsey's report on texas.gov/huntwild/wild/nuisance/feral hogs/. For statistics and reports on feral hog aggression on humans, here are three of the more informative sources: Naomi Millburn on animals.mom.com, David Wilson on quora.com, and Nicholas Bogel-Burroughs on nytimes.com/2019/11/26/us/

texas-woman-killed-feral-hogs.html. The account of Christine Rollins's death is a reconstruction based on media reports.

Page 95 A recent example of rabbit overpopulation is in Victoria, B.C. I've listened to Victorians debate what to do about the rabbits, and opinions seem to vary widely between the extremes of hard-core realism and bunny-loving idealism. I've heard similar debates in Saskatoon between bird lovers and cat owners.

Chapter 13
Heeding the Wolf

Pages 103–111 I can't report on the many recent volumes of wolf research that have emerged in the twenty-first century, but I can point to the books from my own research that were the most enlightening and authoritative. Please see "Further Reading" for more details on these books. I list them here in order of publication:

Douglas Smith and Gary Ferguson, *Decade of the Wolf: Returning the Wild to Yellowstone,* revised edition (Guilford, Connecticut: Lyons Press, 2006).

Ian McCallister, *The Last Wild Wolves: Ghosts of the Great Bear Rainforest* (Vancouver: Greystone Books, 2007).

Paula Wild, *Return of the Wolf: Conflict and Coexistence* (Vancouver: Douglas & McIntyre, 2018).

Rick McIntyre, *The Rise of Wolf 8: Witnessing the Triumph of Yellowstone's Underdog* (Vancouver: Greystone Books, 2019).

Rick McIntyre, *The Reign of Wolf 21: The Saga of Yellowstone's Legendary Druid Pack* (Vancouver: Greystone Books, 2020).

Harold Johnson, *Cry Wolf: Inquest into the True Nature of a Predator* (Regina: University of Regina Press, 2020).

Page 103 For details of the recent slaughter of wolves in Wisconsin, see the April 24, 2021, article in the National Post: nationalpost.com/news/world/hunters-killed-more-than-200-grey-wolves-in-wisconsin-82-more-than-the-states-limit.

Page 109 Herman Melville, *Moby Dick* (London: Penguin Books, 1994; first published in 1851), page 163.

Page 110 This list of wolf sightings in Saskatchewan was compiled partly from my own field notes and partly from those of Mr. Google. My figures for wolf populations in the United States are from the Wolf Conservation Center: nywolf.org/learn/u-s-wolf-populations/.

Pages 111–112 On trophic cascades, see Smith & Ferguson, *Decade of the Wolf*, p. 126.

Page 112 For ecological and zoological research on wolves, see Smith & Ferguson (above), page 126.

Chapter 14
The Cat Came Back

Page 115 Craig Childs, *The Animal Dialogues: Uncommon Encounters in the Wild* (New York: Little, Brown and Company, 2007), pages 108-31.

Pages 117–18, 119–22, 131–32 I am indebted to the following writings (books, articles, chapters, studies) about cougars, many of them quite recent. I list these chronologically.

Kevin Hansen, *Cougar: the American Lion* (Flagstaff: Northland Publishing Company, 1992).

Susan Ewing and Elizabeth Grossman, eds., *Shadowcat: Encountering the American Mountain Lion* (Seattle: Sasquatch Books, 1999).

Craig Childs, "Mountain Lion," in *The Animal Dialogues: Uncommon Encounters in the Wild* (New York: Little, Brown and Company, 2009), pages 47–67.

Paula Wild, *The Cougar: Beautiful, Wild and Dangerous* (Vancouver: Douglas and McIntyre, 2013).

G.A. Bradshaw, "Pumas: Psychological Trauma," in *Carnivore Minds: Who these Fearsome Animals Really Are* (New Haven: Yale University Press, 2017), pages 196–220.

Jim Williams, *Path of the Puma: The Remarkable Resilience of the Mountain Lion* (Santa Clara: Patagonia Books, 2018).

Page 118 On the new evidence of cougars feeding and socializing in groups, see Paula Wild, *The Cougar: Beautiful, Wild and Dangerous*, pages 232–33. See also G.A. Bradshaw, *Carnivore Minds: Who These Fearsome Animals Really Are*, pages 208–09.

Pages 119–20 For the facts on the slaughter of cougars in the United States, see Wayne Pacelle's, "Bullets, Ballots, and Predatory Instincts," in Ewing and Grossman's *Shadowcat: Encountering the American Mountain Lion*, pages 201 and 203.

Page 120 For Hornocker's early study on cougar populations, see Ewing and Grossman, *Shadowcat*, pages 16–17.

Pages 120–21 On recent cougar population dispersals, see Jim Williams's maps in *Path of the Puma*.

Pages 120–21 For records of recent cougar shootings, 1982–2014, see G.A. Bradshaw, *Carnivore Minds*, page 198.

Page 121 On recent cougar population counts, including those done in Canada, see Paula Wild, *The Cougar*, Chapter 13. For American counts, see Ted Williams's essay in Ewing and Grossman, *ShadowCat*, "The Lion's Silent Return."

Page 121–22 For his ecological take on wildlife habitat advocacy, see Jim Williams, *Path of the Puma*, pages 300–02.

Page 122 See Peavy's conclusion to her essay in Ewing and Grossman, *Shadowcat*, page 185.

Pages 122–24 For information on cougar hunting vs. cougar protection in Montana, see Jim Williams, *Path of the Puma*, page 43.

Page 123 Roderick Haig-Brown, *Panther* (London: Collins, 1934). This novel was also issued by an American publisher (Houghton Mifflin) under the title of *Ki-yu*.

Page 127 On the subject of cougar attacks, see Ewing and Grossman's *Shadowcat*, page 205, and especially, see Paula Wild's detailed accounts in chapters four to eleven of *The Cougar*.

Page 129–30 *Saskatoon StarPhoenix*, November 11, 2016.

Page 130 On the subject of alcohol, opioid abuse and Covid 19 in Saskatoon, see Dr. Peter Butt, *Saskatoon StarPhoenix*, June 13, 2020.

Pages 134–137 An earlier version of my four-page anecdote was
published in David Carpenter, *A Hunter's Confession* (Vancouver:
Greystone Books: 2010).

Chapter 15
The Three Bears

Page 142 See Mike Pelton's reflections on bears in Richard Louv,
Our Wild Calling, page 176.

Page 142 A good account of these savage recreations, which
places them in a historical context, is Thomas Babington
Macaulay, *The History of England from the Accession of James II*,
Vol. 1, Sixth Edition, (London: Longman, Green, Brown, and
Longmans, 1850), page 161 and following. I thank Professor
Len Findlay for pointing me to this historical source. Not only is
Findlay a renowned literary scholar, he is no stranger to bears
snuffling around his tent.

Pages 141–142 For a lively Jungian take on this national phobia,
see Robertson Davies's novel, *The Manticore* (Toronto: Macmillan
of Canada, 1972).

Page 146 Charles Russell, *Spirit Bear* (Toronto: Key Porter Books
Limited, 1994).

Pages 148–49 Sid Marty, *The Black Grizzly of Whiskey Creek*
(Toronto: McClelland & Stewart, 2008).

Page 149 Helen Macdonald, *H is for Hawk* (London: Penguin
Books Limited, 2014).

Page 149 John Vaillant, *The Tiger: A True Story of Vengeance and
Survival* (Toronto: Vintage Canada, 2011).

Pages 155–58 Charlie Russell and Maureen Enns, *Grizzly Heart: Living without Fear among the Brown Bears of Kamchatka* (Toronto: Random House of Canada Limited, 2002).

Page 158 My information on the weights attained by brown bears and polar bears comes from Erin McCloskey's *Bear Attacks* (Lone Pine, 2009). In other field guides, the weight estimates of mature brown bears and polar bears are greater. See, for example, James C. Halfpenny, *Scats and Tracks of North America*, pages 174–76; and Fiona Reid, *Mammals of North America*, pages 451–53.

Pages 158–59 There is apparently some disagreement on the subject of polar bear population statistics, the most curiously skewed of which can be found in Elbroch and Rinehart's *Behavior of North American Mammals*, page 133.

Pages 160–61 Stephen Herrero, *Bear Attacks: Their Causes and Avoidance* (Toronto: McClelland & Stewart, 2003 edition).

Pages 160–61 Erin McCloskey, *Bear Attacks in Canada* (Auburn WA: Lone Pine Publishing, 2008).

Page 162–63 There is another version of the Goldilocks tale that has recently caught my eye on television, one of *The Simpsons'* takes on Hallowe'en, and it doesn't end well for Goldilocks. Readers might want to google it.

Chapter 16
Epiphany

Page 165 John Keats, "Ode on a Grecian Urn," *The Norton Anthology of English Literature*, Volume Two, pages 825–27.

Page 169 Roderick Haig-Brown was a renowned naturalist who wrote thirty-one books between 1931 to 1996 in his adopted town of Campbell River, British Columbia. Along with his articles in such magazines as *The Atlantic Monthly* and *The New Yorker,* he was as well known internationally as any writer in Western Canada.

I never met him or his revered wife Ann, but for two long stretches in Campbell River, I lived in the Haig-Brown house as a writer in residence.

Chapter 17
The Cabin that Saskatchewan Built

Pages 175–92 An earlier version of this essay was published in *Western Living*, June 2, 2002, pages 44–50.

Chapter 18
My First Monster

Pages 193–97 I spent many summers as a boy at Lake Wabamun, the setting for this memoir. The largest pike I ever caught there was four and a half pounds (two kilograms). But one winter, I paid a visit to the ice fishers west of our cabin and saw several men admiring a pike that was slightly longer than four feet and weighed very close to thirty pounds (between thirteen and fourteen kilograms).

Epilogue
The Numen

Pages 201 For information on the sixth extinction, see Richard Louv, *Our Wild Calling*, "Introduction" and Chapter 1, "In the Family of Animals"; Stephen Jay Gould, *Wonderful Life: The Burgess*

Shale and the Nature of History, Chapter 5, "Possible Worlds," and also by Gould, *Dinosaur in a Haystack: Reflections in Natural History*, Chapter 12, "Dinosaur in a Haystack," and Chapter 25, "Can We Complete Darwin's Revolution?"; and especially, Elizabeth Kolbert, *The Sixth Extinction: an Unnatural History* (New York: Henry Holt and Company, 2014).

Page 204 James Snider, the World Wildlife Federation's Vice President of Science, Knowledge, and Innovation (WWF-Canada), speaking to news outlets across the country about the Living Planet Report, Canada 2020, Living-Planet-Report-Canada-2020.pdf.

Page 204 See *Saskatoon StarPhoenix*, May 12, 2021, page NP4. Researchers with the Trillion Trees Campaign have discovered that about sixty million hectares of forest all over the planet, from Mongolia to Brazil, have come back since the year 2000. I'd call that a good beginning.

Page 204 Yuval Noah Harari, *Sapiens: A Brief History of Humankind* (Toronto: McClelland & Stewart, Signal Paperback, 2014), page 466.

READING AND VIEWING SHORTLIST

On Dragonflies
G. Hutchings and D. Halstead, *Dragonflies & Damselflies in the Hand: An Identification Guide to Boreal Forest Odonates in Saskatchewan and Adjacent Regions* (Regina: Nature Saskatchewan, 2011).

On Spiders
Paul Hillyard, *The Private Life of Spiders* (Princeton, New Jersey: Princeton University Press, 2011). My knowledge of venomous spiders in North America, South America, and Australia was broadened by this beautifully illustrated book. In addition to Hillyard's wealth of knowledge about spiders, I was much affected by his love for them.

On Snakes
Austin Stevens, *Snakemaster: Wildlife Adventures with the World's Most Dangerous Reptiles* (New York: Skyhorse Publishing, paperback edition, 2019). Stevens's self-proclaiming voice and his weakness for spectacle should have ruined this book, but I found it to be a real page-turner. It brought out the pre-political, adventurous young boy in me.

On Coyotes

For some superbly written journalism on coyotes, see "Coyote," by Craig Childs, in *The Animal Dialogues*, pages 35–46; and "To live and Die in L.A." by David Quammen, *Wild Thoughts from Wild Places*, pages 90–99. Both stories remind me how much the coyote has come to haunt our modern psyches as well as our neighbourhoods.

On Wolves

Ian McAllister, *The Last Wild Wolves: Ghosts of the Rain Forest* (Vancouver: Greystone, 2007). Ian McAllister and his crew (including conservation scientists Chris Darimont and Paul Paquet) worked for seventeen years following two wolf packs in the Great Bear Rain Forest in Northwestern British Columbia. This intimate portrayal of the wolves' domestic and hunting forays, the many startling photographs, and the accompanying DVD make for a groundbreaking study. A heartbreaking and fascinating work.

Douglas Smith and Gary Ferguson, *Decade of the Wolf: Returning the Wild to Yellowstone* (Guilford, Connecticut: Lyons Press, paperback edition, revised and updated, 2012). This is the story of how thirty-one wild wolves from Canada were transported to Yellowstone National Park in 1995–96 by a group of dedicated zoologists and wolf specialists, and how the wolves flourished after their release. What followed was an equally flourishing ecosystem, an adoring army of wolf watchers, and a large contingent of scientists.

Rick McIntyre, *The Rise of Wolf 8: Witnessing the Triumph of Yellowstone's Underdog* (Vancouver: Greystone Books, 2019) and

The Reign of Wolf 21: the Saga of Yellowstone's Legendary Druid Pack (Vancouver: Greystone Books, 2020). These two books are part of the Alpha Wolves of Yellowstone series. McIntyre is an alpha observer among wolf watchers. For years, he stuck with these wolves and reported on the details of their lives as they grew into local legends.

Paula Wild, *Return of the Wolf: Conflict and Coexistence* (Vancouver: Douglas and McIntyre, 2018). Paula Wild's broad study of wolves takes us from the old world with all its mythologizing of wolves to the new world, where people are divided between fear and hatred of wolves and an ever-growing love for them. She is of the latter persuasion; she warns us to be smart and wary in their territory, but she is just as vigilant on behalf of these admirable carnivores.

Harold R. Johnson, *Cry Wolf: Inquest in the True Nature of a Predator* (Regina: University of Regina Press, 2020). Harold Johnson takes a different stand from Paula Wild—who demonstrates a great love for wolves—and from McCallister, McIntyre, Smith, and Ferguson, who defend the wolf against all comers. Johnson takes us from a northern mining camp, where a young employee has been killed, into the courtroom and an inquest to tell his story. In doing so, Johnson reminds us that, although the wolves have been senselessly victimized by gun-loving nimrods, they are to be respected and treated warily by us. He has much to say about how to avoid habituating wolves.

On Cougars
Kevin Hansen, *Cougar: The American Lion* (Flagstaff: Northland Publishing Company, 1992). This book is a resource for scientific

data on cougars living primarily in the United States. It covers everything from skeletal structure and anatomy to population dynamics, distribution, and international habitats.

Susan Ewing and Elizabeth Grossman, eds., *ShadowCat: Encountering the American Mountain Lion* (Seattle: Sasquatch Books, 1999). This book is a collection of essays that offer an excellent variety of reflections on the plight of cougars in the United States. Some of these pieces are authoritative studies, but most are personal encounters. An informative, exciting read.

Craig Childs, "Mountain Lion," in *The Animal Dialogues: Uncommon Encounters in the Wild* (New York: Little, Brown and Company, 2007), pages 47–67. This chapter is a riveting memoir about Childs's encounter with a cougar.

Paula Wild, *The Cougar: Beautiful, Wild and Dangerous* (Vancouver: Douglas & McIntyre, 2013). Like her book, *Return of the Wolf: Conflict and Coexistence*, this study of the cougar in North America contains a wealth of scholarship, current information, and hair-raising stories, many of them set in Canada. Wild has much to say about cougar attacks on humans and how to be safe in cougar country.

Jim Williams, *Path of the Puma* (Santa Clara: Patagonia Books, 2018). Williams is a wildlife biologist, ecologist, and conservationist who, for several decades, has followed cougars through the snow and the mountains from the Montana Rockies to the wilds of Patagonia. He divides this book between these two regions and has much to say about their restless journeys through the Americas. G.A. Bradshaw, below, is acutely aware of how cougars have been slaughtered and extirpated from their traditional habitats; Jim Williams is more optimistic and argues exuberantly for habitat conservation, citing some heartening examples.

G.A. Bradshaw, *Carnivore Minds: Who these Fearsome Animals Really Are* (New Haven, Connecticut: Yale University Press, 2017). Bradshaw is the director of an animal sanctuary, and in her book she speaks as both scientist and science reporter. I'm tempted to call her a wild animal psychologist, but she wears several hats and defies easy classification. Bradshaw speaks sometimes in the academic diction of the social scientist, sometimes in the voice of the neuroscientist, and sometimes in the words of a compassionate activist for wild carnivores.

Note especially "Pumas: Psychological Trauma," in *Carnivore Minds*, pages 196–220.

On Bears
Charlie Russell and Maureen Enns, *Grizzly Heart: Living Without Fear Among the Brown Bears of Kamchatka* (Toronto: Random House of Canada Limited, 2002). Russell and Enns wrote this volume with assistance from Fred Stenson. This compelling book is the story of Russell and Enns's involvement with brown bears in Kamchatka—especially the three bear cubs they rescued from a crate and raised up for a year like foster children. Russell highlights the conflict over hunters eager to kill brown bears for fun and profit, and bear-loving environmentalists who want to let them roam free. This is the most absorbing, heartfelt book on bears that I've ever read.

Recently, I came upon a hopeful sign of bear–human interaction, a daytime television show on the Animal Planet Network (sometimes on the Knowledge Network and the Discovery Channel) that I have begun to watch entitled *Wild Bear Rescue*. It features Angelika Langen, her husband Peter Langen, and the dedicated staff of the Northern Lights Wildlife Society in Smithers, British Columbia. Most of the caregivers are women. They work to rehabilitate injured or otherwise at-risk bear cubs, fatten them up, and then release them back into the wild. The aim is not to habituate bears but to get them healthy and independent. There is a scene from one of the episodes (used in their trailer ads) in which Angelika calls the cubs for their dinner. In seconds, the cubs appear, perhaps fifteen of them, gleefully galloping to their bowls of food. Imagine, a stampeding herd of happy bear cubs. Angelika and her staff have been feeding, nursing, cuddling, and occasionally scolding these bears to straighten up and fly right until they are ready for their graduation ceremony, which involves jumping from a metal container in the back of a truck. Back to the woods they go, strengthened by the force of maternal devotion.

BOOKS AND FILMS FOR
GENERAL INTEREST

Mark Elbroch and Kurt Rinehart, *Behavior of North American Mammals* (New York: Houghton Mifflin Harcourt Publishing Company; Peterson Reference Guide, 2011). This volume is essential reading for anyone interested in the everyday lives of wild mammals, especially in the United States.

For maps and other quick references I found Fiona Reid's *Mammals of North America* (New York: Houghton Mifflin, 4th edition, 2006) quite helpful.

For tracking information, I found James C. Halfpenny's *Scats and Tracks of North America* (Guilford, Connecticut: Rowman & Littlefield, 2008) the most helpful of several similar studies.

Richard Louv, *Our Wild Calling: How Connecting with Animals can Transform Our Lives—and Save Theirs* (Chapel Hill: Algonquin Books, 2019). Richard Louv works to connect us more deeply with threatening creatures such as rattlesnakes, as do his interviewees, Gordon Burghardt and Harry Greene. Their observations on reptile behaviour take us to the heart of critical anthropomorphism, which is what G.A. Bradshaw (see above) is all about. Louv's book is a gathering place for current progressive views on how to understand wild carnivores. Critical Anthropomorphism starts with objective science and gains a depth of understanding through intuition, or what what Louv calls "imaginative identification." As a consciousness raiser arguing for closer communion between animals and people, Louv is a Noah for the twenty-first century. He introduces us to the work of so many inspired naturalists, animal psychologists, anthrozoologists, wild animal advocates, ecologists, and philosophers, that reading his book will urge many of us to become activists in the cause of reconnecting with wild animals.

Helen Macdonald, *H is for Hawk* (Toronto: Penguin Canada Books, 2014). Macdonald's honest and penetrating book is a true-life account of her passionate attachment to a goshawk at a time in her life when she is lost and grieving over the death of her father. This attachment to a predator bird is not merely sentimental or neurotic, but soul-searchingly empathetic, crazy, and wise. She is almost always aware of just how obsessive her love is for her ferocious little hawk, but, at the same time, she witnesses a miracle of transcendence in which she moves at last beyond the stasis of grief. A breathtaking read.

Peter Godfrey-Smith, *Other Minds: the Octopus, the Sea, and the Deep Origins of Consciousness* (New York: Farrar, Straus and Giroux, 2016). The author dives down into the mysteries of intelligence and the origins of consciousness in cephalopods and sapiens. In spite of his very impressive credentials as a scientist-philosopher, he strikes me as more scientist than philosopher. I found his scientific inquiries into the evolution of cognition in various organisms heavy going. But when his narrative switches to his observations of octopuses in the ocean and in captivity, this book really takes off. His stories (and the accompanying photos) take us into some startling revelations about how intelligent octopuses really are.

Craig Foster, *My Octopus Teacher* (Netflix original film documentary, 2020; directed by Pippa Ehrlich and James Reed). Scuba diver and filmmaker Craig Foster spends a year scuba diving in a kelp forest near Cape Town. In the process of documenting the perilous daily life of an octopus, he comes to love this resourceful animal and to feel protective of it. A surprisingly moving documentary.

David Quammen, *Monster of God: The Man-Eating Predator in the Jungles of History and the Mind* (New York: W.W. Norton and Company, Inc., 2003). This tome is about apex predators throughout the world that have terrorized people from time immemorial: bears, crocodiles, lions, tigers, and many others. Quammen not only seeks out these predators, he also explores the shadows they have cast on our psyches and their godlike status among various groups of people that revere them. These animals are living marvels.

John Vaillant, *The Tiger: a True Story of Vengeance and Survival* (Toronto: Vintage Canada, 2011). This adventurous and rigourously researched tale takes place in the Russian far east, in the Bikin Valley north of Vladivostok, not far from the area explored earlier by David Quammen in *Monsters of God*. It's the story of a rare Siberian tiger and the people who lived harmoniously (or otherwise) with the tiger in its territory. Written with great insight into Russian history and politics, this story is impelled by a hunt for a tiger bent on revenge. Those of us who take seriously the plight of endangered animals and their vanishing habitat may find themselves rooting for the tiger.

David Attenborough, *A Life on our Planet* (Netflix documentary, 2020). David Attenborough has put together so many absorbing film documentaries on nature that I hesitate to name any one in particular. But if you are passionate about protecting and restoring the wild habitat that is home to so many wild creatures, you might start with his film *A life on our Planet*, which follows his life as a naturalist from early boyhood to old age. Attenborough, among other things, is a strong advocate of rewilding disturbed habitats around our planet.

David Carpenter is the author of fourteen books, including nonfiction, several novels (most recently *The Gold*), short story collections, a collection of novellas (*Welcome to Canada*), and one volume of poetry. He is also the editor of the three volume *Literary History of Saskatchewan* and the *The Education of Augie Merasty*. He has received several Saskatchewan Book Awards, including Book of the Year for *A Hunter's Confession*, as well as National and Western Magazine Awards for his magazine writing. In 2015 he was the recipient of the Kloppenburg Award for Literary Excellence, and in 2018 he was awarded an Honorary Doctorate from the University of Saskatchewan, where he taught for two decades. He still spends a lot of time in the bush.

Feb